READY OR NOT HERE IT COMES

Ready or Not Here It Comes: Incredibly Simple Tips to an
Awesome Life for You and the Planet

ISBN 13: 978-0-9846952-0-1

Book Design by custom-book-tique.com
Cover Design by Alyssa Aquino

For bulk order prices or any other inquiries, please contact
starsong@prodigy.net.mx

www.chrissausser.com

READY OR NOT HERE IT COMES

Incredibly Simple Tips to an Awesome Life for You and the Planet

CHRIS SAUSSER

LUMINESCENCE PUBLISHING

To my mom and dad –
I wish you were here.

CONTENTS

A Grateful Heart

I want to thank my sister, Ellen, for her tremendous support always, and in general, putting up with my shenanigans! Thanks to my daughter, Alyssa, computer whiz kid, photographer, cover designer, title-thinker-upper and lover of my writing.

Much gratitude to my friend, Alexandra Bondarew, for her enthusiasm for each chapter, her wise advice and the time she dedicated to reading. A big hug goes to Laura Bonilla and all her positive thoughts and great ideas. Kudos goes to Pat Kerr, for her generous heart in editing the book. Thanks to my Kindle guru, Michael Sheridan and his skill and wise counsel. Much appreciation goes to Maggie Pagratis, for her care and professionalism in book design. And thanks to my feathered serpent, Jorge Alejandro Garcia, for his invaluable expertise with my web page and other delicate media matters.

I am utterly grateful to be a part of this incredible creation, planet and humanity. And final thanks goes to my guides and angels on the other side who have inspired and supported me from the beginning.

PREFACE

It is clear that the planet along with the human race is undergoing an unprecedented shift in energy, vibration and ultimately, consciousness.

I have been studying the spiritual side of life for 32 years. I have read hundreds of books, traveled to sacred spots around the planet, taken classes and gone to workshops. I work with energy healing, flower essences and crystals. I have had the great luxury of time. Unfortunately, time has run out. There is no more time for lengthy studies or soul searching.

There is only the need for clear intent to harness our soul energy and assist this shift in consciousness as foretold by soothsayers and the Mayan calendar. You can feel it in the air - it's not business as usual. Who could say that they can't feel the difference after the massive earthquakes in Haiti, Chile, New Zealand and Japan? A massive volcanic eruption in Iceland held European air traffic hostage for almost a month. Who can deny the impact of the Mideast countries' frantic battle for independence from cruel, despotic rulers? Who can close their eyes to the cyber web around the planet uniting us in split-second technology? We are not in Kansas anymore, Dorothy.

I have acquired much information in my years of study and I want to share it with you. I want to cut to the chase. I want to be Cliff's Notes for The Shift we are in the midst of right now. I want to point you to valuable resources you can access quickly, easily and in many cases, without cost. Some of the information suggests ways to optimize your health in order to maximize your ability to absorb the energy embracing the planet. Use the information that resonates with you, and anything else put aside.

It is the moment to choose sides. You are part of the problem or part of the solution. You want to evolve or you want to stay stuck in the same old stagnant patterns of existence that have stunted our growth as incredible light beings filled with love.

It is time. Read this book and do just one small thing you find in these pages and I guarantee that your life will change in amazing ways. The lives of the people around you will change as well. The ripple continues on.

HOW TO USE THIS BOOK

Please do use this book as a tool! Don't just read it, do it. Do the meditations, go to the websites, download the freebies online. Mom always told you not to mark up your books, but I'm giving you permission to underline, mark it up, bend the corners, tear out pages and tape them to your mirror or carry them in your pocket or your purse. Make this book part of your life and shift your energy along with the planet. Don't go, nice idea, I'll do it someday. Do it today and embrace the energy!

1

Love is all you need.

The Beatles

When I was eleven years old, my mom gave me a small Lucite keychain. On one side a tiny flower was imbedded in the piece and on the other side it said 'God Is Love.' I adored that key chain, and on some level I knew the words were true. I was raised a Catholic and attended parochial school. I was invested in all the ritual and dogma that the Catholic religion had to offer. But I really believed the words on my keychain, even though I had not been taught that at school.

I was taught that even though my mother was a wonderful woman, she was not Catholic and so she would be denied heaven, maybe even go to hell. I was taught the disgrace of original sin and the multitude of sins both venial and mortal that would accrue grave punishment in the afterlife. But love entered little into the mix.

Fast forward to my adult years when I began my quest to really figure out life. What was going on? Why were we here? As I mentioned before, I spent years searching, reading and experiencing. The funny thing is that no matter what I read or where I looked, it was always the same answer. Love. Just love. I would have expected to read all kinds of things in the many sources I researched, with many different answers. But it was love. Only love.

And I am not talking about sissy love, romantic, easy love. I am talking about unconditional love. I am talking about the love that unites us all in unity consciousness. I am talking about love without judgment for every human being on this planet. It is very simple – love. But it is also the most difficult thing to do. You must love the unlovable and turn your cheek when you have been wounded. It is not for the faint of heart.

You must love Adolf Hitler. Yes, that's correct, Adolf Hitler. You must not condone the heinous atrocities he committed, but you must love that glimmer of God in his soul, and forgive him. Right now you are saying, 'She's crazy, love Adolf Hitler! She's a nut job.' But a seed has been planted. On some level you know I am right. And when you least expect it, that crazy thought will come to you – love Adolf Hitler? And that includes loving the jerk that cut you off in traffic this morning, or the person in the next cubicle at work who drives you crazy, and yes, even that smelly homeless man that you passed on the street this morning. They all started out as lovely, sweet babies with charming smiles and chubby cheeks. How they progressed in life on their journey is not for us to judge, only to recognize the God source within. Simple, yes. Easy, no.

When I hear about a pedophile or murderer in the news, I forgive that person and send him love and light, that his spirit may use the light or not, as appropriate. We are all in this third dimensional classroom together, learning to Be. Some are at university level, while others may be kindergarteners. We must accept where everyone is in their evolution.

I was so disappointed recently when people cheered in the streets with such hatred and gloating that Bin Laden was dead. I forgave him and sent him love and light on his transition. Yes, you must even love Bin Laden – and you know this is so. No, I am not a goody-two-shoes or a saint. But I get it. I know love is the answer. We are all One. If people don't get it soon, I am afraid the human race will have to learn that lesson the hard way.

So I smile to myself sometimes that I searched for the answer to life for over 32 years in so many far-flung places and in so many books, when I had it all along in my little Lucite keychain – God Is Love.

2

Your Thoughts Create Reality

Jane Roberts -Seth Speaks

Around 1976 I read a channeled book called Seth Speaks in which the entity Seth held forth on many topics over hundreds of pages. The information was so detailed about parallel realities, parallel universes, creation and other heady material, I decided no one could make it up. Though it is quite commonplace to believe now that thoughts do create reality, at the time it was quite an amazing statement.

Quantum physics has now proven that what a researcher believes about an experiment will actually influence the outcome of the experiment. In his book, The Divine Matrix, Gregg Braden cites several experiments which actually prove this point. So what a researcher believes will happen in the experiment, will actually create that outcome in the experiment. The possibilities are staggering.

More importantly, Braden explained in one of his conferences that there are two satellites 18,000 miles from the planet which do nothing but monitor the planetary magnetic field twenty-four hours a day. When researchers were checking past data, they saw an incredible week-long increase in the earth's magnetic field. When they traced the data back, they found that the magnetic field of the earth skyrocketed within ten minutes of the first plane hitting the World Trade Center on September 11, 2001, the time it took for the images to be shown around the world. The energy lasted a week. So not only do our thoughts create reality, but so do our feelings. The shock, horror, love, grief and compassion that flowed from humanity around the planet was an energy powerful enough to spike the earth's magnetic field.

Amazing. Can you imagine if that same energy were harnessed through a worldwide meditation or prayer? And there are many people on the planet doing that right now, holding group meditations simultaneously around our planet. Many of these events take place on the equinoxes, solstices or other significant days. Hundreds of people participated in energy sessions after the earthquake in Japan to send light, love and healing to the Japanese people and the nuclear reactors.

Quantum physics is melding religion and science, the gray area where God exists in the spaces between the smallest imaginable units of matter. So, apart from monitoring our thoughts and feelings, we also need to be mindful of the words coming out of our mouths. If you go around constantly saying that this is a 'pain in the butt and that is a pain in the butt,' you're going to get hemorrhoids! Yes, that's the way it works.

Every single thing in creation is made up of energy – and that energy is alive and vibrates. Some things vibrate at a rate which is dense, thick, heavy, slow, while other things vibrate rapidly, at unimaginable speeds. With intent, your own energy can manifest results in your life. You will see it when you believe it. Watch the movie "What the Bleep Do We Know" for much more about energy and manifestation.

Have you heard of yogis who bi-locate or produce objects out of thin air? What about Jesus when he fed his followers with baskets and baskets of food? They stepped outside of limiting third dimensional mind-sets and with intent and belief used energy to create their desired outcome. Conviction is what makes it happen.

When my daughter was four years old, we were building our house. Visiting the construction site one evening, she said she was going to bring me a heart-shaped rock. I smiled to myself and thought that she would be kept occupied for a while. In less than a minute she came back to me with a perfect heart-shaped rock. I was astonished. Her conviction that she would find a heart, created exactly that. It was a small reminder from the universe.

So, what it comes down to is that we can create what we want on this planet. We can heal Gaia. We can create a society filled with a better life and incredible opportunities. We need to unite – unity consciousness – and start using our minds for more than tv, video games or fear-filled scenarios. Start today. Start right this moment. Take two or three slow, deep breaths. Close your eyes for a moment and then think of the world you want - always in the positive. Think of peace versus ending war. Think of unlimited agricultural abundance versus ending starvation. Or think of changes in your personal life. You get the idea. But do it, right now. It only takes a minute or two. And apart from creating, I bet you feel a bit better than you did a moment ago. So try it several times throughout the day.

Try it for twenty-four hours. I dare you. Be mindful of what you think, feel and say. Turn off that monkey mind that is always going blah, blah, blah. The ego loves to be in charge and doesn't want there to be any significant change. So that monkey mind is always blathering about other people, their imagined motives, scary ideas about the future and unproductive thoughts about the past. The moment of power is right now, this very moment that you are holding this book. Eckhart Tolle so eloquently states this in his book, A New Earth. Oprah recognized the importance of this book and featured it as one of her book club selections. She even went so far as to have an internet class with Tolle, which reached millions of people.

Take the dare. Take back your power as the creator of your life and ultimately the planet. Accept the responsibility. And see what a difference twenty-four hours can make.

3

Happy Is As Happy Does

Happiness and gratitude will get you the golden ring. Once again, it's simple. If you are happy and grateful you will vibrate at a higher frequency where you can more easily create your reality. The trick is to maintain that quickening of vibration. I know, I know. Who can be happy and thankful all day when the baby is crying, when foreclosure is hanging over your head, when your mate or a family member has cancer, when work just sucks and on and on?

Well, it's like love, it's simple but not easy. You have to work at it and develop little tricks that will help the process. The easier side of the equation is to be thankful. When you start thinking about it, there are a million things to be thankful for. Be thankful when you open your eyes in the morning that you have another day to live on this beautiful planet. Be thankful for the electricity that powers your home and all the employees that make the electricity possible. Be thankful for the water that comes right into your home. Be thankful for breakfast, whatever that may be. Be thankful for transportation, even if it is the city bus. Be thankful for the shimmering raindrops on the window, for the laughter of your children, for your furry friends. You get the idea. But the trick is to do it frequently throughout the day. If you can go so far as to keep a gratitude journal, it's even better. But if your life is just too full for that, then at least think the thoughts. It's only a second or two. If you need to, set your watch alarm so it beeps on the hour and give thanks at that moment. Or do it when the phone rings, or when you are at a stoplight. But it's important to do it.

Then, once you are in the habit of saying thanks, hopefully you will be happier because you recognize how blessed you are. If that hasn't quite done the trick, you need to decide what puts a smile on your face. Is there a certain song you can blare while you are driving that will just make you so happy? How about a memory of one of the best times of your life? Singing really loud? You have to figure out what to have in your bag of tricks. But do it right away, no matter what, and you will begin to feel different.

Then you need to learn to deal with all the things that happen throughout the day that can just wipe all that happiness and gratitude right off the slate. Acknowledge them, thank them for showing you something that you need to be aware of – something inside of you that you are projecting that attracts those things like a magnet. Then release them, transmute them. In an instant just give them up to God or the universe to be turned into pure energy.

When you start screaming at your kids, stop and transmute that energy. Just let it go and breathe. When you go ballistic at work, stop, let it go and imagine it dissolve into energy. When the store clerk is angry and rude, send that energy to God. That's why everything is much easier if you can be in the moment.

It seems like hocus pocus. But it isn't. It really works. I live it every day. And although my life circumstances have been far from idyllic, I feel great and I attract many gifts from the universe.

When I was little I saw the Disney movie Pollyanna. I will never forget how she always looked on the bright side. She played the Glad Game. Pollyanna's minister father taught her to find something to be glad about at the end of each day. I remember when she showed the crabby old Mr. Pendergast the delight of hanging glass crystals in his windows to create rainbows throughout his home. I know it sounds really corny and lame, but take a page from Pollyanna.

4

'Let there be light,' and there was light.

Genesis 1:3

Photons are subatomic particles of light, the quantum of electromagnetic light, which originate in the core of the sun. The sun is more active than ever with solar eruptions and solar flares sending more photon energy through space to our planet. You could say things are heating up. Esoteric wisdom says this energy is assisting with the shift in consciousness that we are undergoing right now. The energy raises the vibration of the planet and allows us to manifest more quickly. Author Alberto Villoldo says in his book The Four Insights, that we are evolving into Homo luminous, radiating light on a cellular and energetic level.

Intensified energy is entering into earth's atmosphere right now and it can make us feel like we are living in a pressure cooker. I am convinced that what is happening now on both a personal and planetary level is due to the massive infusion of energy to the planet. The energy influences countries to finally want to throw off the rule of despots and dictators no matter the consequences. Many people who have no idea why they feel the way they do, commit acts of desperation and seeming madness.

Knowing that this energy exists gives us an advantage. It explains why things are happening in our daily lives and in the news and it allows us to harness this very potent energy for positive results. It is important to stay in the moment as much as possible. If you can do it every waking hour, that would be great. If that is too ambitious, do it as much as possible. Remember that the more you do it, the more it will become a habit for you.

That state of awareness is also a place of power. By staying in the moment you can be proactive and not reactive. It allows you to see opportunities from the universe as they arise and it makes it much easier to focus and use intent and a positive mind to magnetize what your thoughts, feelings and words are creating. You control the energy rather than having the energy control you. By trying this even for a day, I am sure you will notice a shift in your energy, your life and quite likely in the lives of those around you.

5

Energetic Housecleaning

Chakra is a Sanskrit word which means 'wheel.' Everyone has seven chakras, or energy centers aligned in the head and down the spine which connect our physical body to our energetic bodies. We have many more minor chakras located throughout the body. The life force infuses our bodies with energy via the chakras. The brain and our nervous system are heavily influenced by the chakras, as is our endocrine system.

One of the important things about the chakras is that they store stuck emotions and feelings not only from this lifetime, but from past lifetimes as well. If your chakras are clogged with old, useless patterns, source energy is not able to circulate freely in the body, affecting health and emotional well-being.

There are many techniques to cleanse and balance the chakras and many healers who specialize in working with crystals and gemstones, sound, color, light and bodywork to cleanse and energize the energy centers. You can also work on your own chakras with meditation cds created specifically for chakra cleansing, which use guided visualization. Energy therapist Carol Tuttle, www.chakrahealing.com, offers a chakra test to see what shape your chakras are in. At www.sourcevibrations.com, you can download a free audio chakra tuner. Healing sound pioneer and composer Steven Halpern, www.innerpeacemusic.com, offers his classic Chakra Suite cd to harmonize and balance the chakras.

The most important thing to know is that cleansing and balancing the chakras is an ongoing process. The chakras have layers and layers of psychic debris built up over lifetimes and usually need several sessions to really get clear. Just think of cleaning silver and you rub and you rub and you rub and the rag is still black, until you finally see the true glimmer of the metal.

Many years ago I was having a massage with a very gifted healer. As he was working with deep tissue technique on my abdomen, I flashed to a place where I was being held by soldiers in heavy coats and boots that seemed to be either Russian or German. I couldn't make out exactly the time period, but I was pregnant and being repeatedly and painfully kicked in the stomach by the soldiers. I knew that I had lost the baby and possibly my life, although I was not sure. The flash was brief, but very real and intense. I had never experienced anything like that before. Up until that time I had recurring ovarian cysts, one of which burst and required emergency surgery. Once I had experienced the psychic flashback, I never had another cyst.

Cleansing your chakras is as important to your health as brushing your teeth. As soon as you begin to work with it, you will feel a difference and you will be better equipped to use the incoming photon energy. Start today.

6

'I can't express anger ...
I grow a tumor instead.'

Woody Allen – Manhattan

Woody had it right. Unexpressed emotion is the cause of illness. Now you're saying, here we go again – she's saying crazy stuff. What about germs, viruses and diseases?

The body is an incredibly complex organism with trillions of cells running myriad processes every second of every day. Given exactly what it needs, the body is capable of cleansing, healing and balancing itself and maintaining vibrant health and well-being. Where the problem comes in, is when we can't manage our emotions. Remember that emotions have a vibration. When we are stressed out, afraid, angry or sad, negative vibrations are created in our etheric energy body which surrounds our physical body. If we can deal with the emotions at that level, with healing modalities including energy work, breath work, flower essences, the Emotional Freedom Technique and countless others, the energy can be released before it has a chance to cause a diseased state within our physical body.

Some situations, like relationship or work issues can carry on for years. The negative vibrations created by these are present on the etheric level but when we don't handle the energy on the etheric level, it can take years for the imbalance to manifest on the physical level.

I believe that cancer begins in just that way, that there is some situation that has festered for years, possibly buried deep within the psyche that a person doesn't even remember – that the subconscious keeps hidden. I was told by a healer that breast cancer occurs when a woman does not nurture herself, when she is so busy taking care of everyone else in so many ways, that she doesn't do the small nurturing things that reflect her self-love and self worth. Dr. Bernie Siegel's book, Love, Medicine and Miracles, talks about the distinct mind-body relationship in his surgical practice. He found that when one of his patients had a massive heart attack, the man had just experienced a painful divorce and his heart was literally 'broken.' Possibly someone with throat cancer has not been able to give voice to true feelings, or a person who finds it difficult to let go, gets kidney disease. I know someone who did not feel supported by his family and he experienced terrible back pain. He couldn't carry the load alone any more. Sometimes people get sick because they simply want attention or some tender loving care. It may seem an over simplification of a complex issue, but I believe there is a definite connection in these instances.

Look to your own life. You feel out of control, or out of balance, maybe not grounded and you fall and twist your ankle. When I am sick or I injure myself, I always look to my life circumstances to understand why I attracted that particular illness or situation into my life. Louise Hay in her book You Can Heal Your Life, has a pages-long list of symptoms and possible emotional causes. The times I have consulted the list about myself or a family member have been very telling, with more than a grain of truth. During the healing process, it's paramount to find the real reason for imbalance and illness. If only the symptoms are treated the illness will recur or another imbalance will take hold in the body. Also included here is the aging process. An emotionally happy and balanced individual will usually age much more slowly and without serious illness than a person who is depressed, disillusioned or unhappy. By recognizing the underlying cause of illness and addressing it specifically, true healing may take place.

7

100% Natural

I know I just belabored the point that illness begins on the emotional level. But now I need to tell you why we still need to be diligent about what goes in and around our bodies.

When our emotions are in check, we are healthy as our immune systems are strong. With a strong immune system we can fend off bacteria, viruses, toxins and anything else that might be damaging to our health. When our vibration is lowered due to emotional imbalances, including stress, our immune system is not as strong. It cannot combat the onslaught of biological and environmental hazards. Our bodies also have to deal with free radicals, atoms with an unpaired electron which are by-products of cellular processes and environmental toxins. Free radicals are damaging, cause disease and ultimately, aging. This explanation is highly simplified, but is enough that you get the idea. I always picture the free radicals as terrorists running rampant in my body. Antioxidants and nutrients in our food, check the production of free radicals and offset their damaging effects.

The very best way to get antioxidants is by eating a diet of fresh foods that have high antioxidant levels. Vegetables and fruits offer the best antioxidants with blueberries, goji berries and acai berries having some of the very highest antioxidant levels. Right now, many manufacturers list 'antioxidants' prominently on their labels. But if you are tempted to buy a product because of its antioxidant content, check the label carefully. So much of what is on the supermarket shelves is riddled with artificial flavors, artificial colors, hidden sugar, hidden salt and other chemical compounds that cause havoc with our immune system. In fact you should always read food labels until you are familiar with all the products that you normally use.

Take a stand. Just put down the package if it has bogus ingredients. Don't eat garbage, don't feed your family garbage. Because that is what all that stuff that has artificial ingredients and chemical fillers is – garbage. Companies use all those disgusting ingredients because they are cheaper and provide them with higher profits. Or because they are chemically addictive to the body, especially for children, and they create junk food junkies. Sounds harsh, but it's true. Do you remember the movie Network from 1976, where Peter Finch is shouting out the window 'I'm mad as hell and I'm not going to take it anymore?' That's how I feel right now. Why do you think so many people in America, including children, are overweight, obese, disease-ridden, diabetic and have heart disease and cancer? Garbage. If we stop buying garbage, they will stop making garbage. Hit them where it hurts, in the financial report.

My daughter was regularly getting huge hives and we were confounded as to the reason. We would go over what she had eaten that day with a fine tooth comb, analyzing every bite. No, it was all something that she had eaten before without a problem. We ended up going to an allergist who suggested to us that the artificial color yellow was highly allergic to many children. We thought back and bingo! She drank orange soda on those days when she had gotten the hives. I started reading labels more closely and was astonished to find how many products had artificial yellow coloring in them, strange products that you never would imagine contained yellow coloring. I have been reading labels ever since. Do it, you will be surprised. And if the grocery store has issues, think about restaurants. The only thing you can do is to buy and order natural where possible, organic even better. Try to be creative and cook your own meals. If your time is just stretched too thin, read the labels in the store so you purchase the least toxic product possible for you and your family. Oh, did I say toxic? That's because all those products with Frankenstein ingredients are toxic.

Do you know what body burden is? Body burden is the number of different chemicals found in the body at any one time. Most people have traces of over 100 chemicals when tested. Newborns have been found to have almost as many, having been passed the chemicals through the placenta. Scary, huh? CNN's Anderson Cooper was tested and he couldn't believe that he had over 100 toxic chemicals in his body. You probably won't be having the test anytime soon as it costs thousands of dollars to do the individual testing for so many chemicals. That's why it is imperative, as closely as possible, to guard your exposure to unnecessary chemicals and additives.

Watch out for chemicals for cleaning, pesticides and fertilizers. All are toxic, unless you are using the new natural brands. Target carries a whole line of environmentally friendly cleaning products under the Method brand name. People think that if aerosol bug sprays are on the supermarket shelves, that they are safe. Think again. If you want to be proactive go to the Pesticide Action Network's website www.panna.org and sign up for their newsletter. You will be amazed that such highly toxic substances are used around the world, and you will have the chance for your voice to be heard through their petitions and campaigns. Another source for information is the Organic Consumers Association, www.organicconsumers.org.

Another way we encounter chemicals is through the use of personal products like shampoos, conditioners, deodorant and make-up. Sodium lauryl sulfate is found in so many soaps, shampoos and other products and is highly toxic. That's only one of the many chemicals on the labels of personal care products. So if you don't want to spend half your life reading tiny print on jars and bottles, you need to buy natural and organic products. Many companies take pride in producing a line of products that perform without toxic ingredients. Whole Foods has a wide array of products for every facet of your life. Trader Joe's – if you are lucky enough to have one in your city – has unusual and inventive foods with natural ingredients on the label and low prices to boot. If they can do it, any manufacturer can do it. It just takes creativity and integrity. Amazon.com offers lots of natural personal care products, as does Vitaminshoppe.com. Brands to look for include Kiss My Face, Aubrey Organics, Puritan Pride, Mill Creek, Home Health, Tom's of Maine and the Jason brand. And don't forget to drop in at your local natural health food store. Buy local, buy small when possible. Shop the farmers' market near your home and support local farmers and get great food that goes from field to table.

Another thing that is really toxic without people realizing it is dry- cleaning. Super toxic. Imagine, clothes soaked with chemical and then you wear it against your skin – your largest organ – all day long. There are businesses that now use a new, environmentally friendly procedure. Seek them out or just don't buy clothes that you need to have dry-cleaned. And when you are fighting mosquitoes, use a natural product with essential oils. Anything with DEET will kill the mosquitoes, but it's a killer for you, too, especially children.

You have to pick your battles. I don't expect for you to change overnight in every aspect of your being, but be aware. Be conscious. Know that you have a choice. Know that you have the power to change your life, exactly as you want and at your own pace. Know that how you spend your money, where and on what products does matter and does make a difference. Think about yourself and your family and about the healthiest option. And as you begin to be more aware and make changes bit by bit, it will be easier and you will flow from one change to another as if you are lazily floating downstream in an inner tube on a sunny day. It can be that easy.

8

Clean Machine

As I've said, it's necessary to have a clean machine so you stay healthy even when you're not vibrating at an optimum level. Apart from the obvious you are what you eat, there are many other factors you need to consider to keep your energy field clear and strong.

Make sure the water you are drinking is healthy. Older buildings may have lead pipes and if your city is putting chlorine and fluoride, both toxic, in the water, you really need to have a filter on your tap, or buy one of the pitchers like Brita that has a filter in it. Fluoride is a really interesting story.

With heavy aluminum processing in the 1940s, there was a tremendous amount of fluoride – a processing by-product – piling up. The government was pressuring companies to handle the waste. Somehow the idea that fluoride was beneficial to dental health was dreamed up and the aluminum industry poured heavy money into research. Researchers coming up with findings that indicated fluoride was anything less than beneficial, lost their funding. Then the aluminum industry pulled the scam of the century and started charging for its waste to be used for 'dental health.' I am surprised that they didn't try to sell the government the Brooklyn Bridge.

So we have been exposed to highly toxic fluoride for about six decades, mainly through our water supply, supposedly protecting our teeth against cavities. It has never been approved by the FDA. Although many countries also began using fluoride during the 50s and 60s, most European countries have removed fluoride from their water supplies.

Current research indicates that fluoride damages the nervous system, causes hypothyroidism by depleting iodine in the body, causes kidney disease, immune deficiency and weakens bones. India has parts of their country that have so much naturally occurring fluoride in the ground that they need to take fluoride out of their groundwater. The population in that area has sustained heavy damage to the nervous system and bone deformities.

In Australia, hundreds of kangaroos died last year from fluoride poisoning at a location adjacent to an aluminum smelter. Recently, there was a fluoride spill at a water treatment facility in Rock Island, Illinois. Emergency responders had to wear hazmat gear. The fluoride burned through the cement in the parking lot. Does that sound like something you want to have in your drinking water or be brushing on your teeth twice a day? Try to find toothpaste without fluoride. Tom's of Maine, Burt's Bees, Kiss My Face and Dr. Ken's all offer fluoride-free toothpaste.

The worst part right now is that the majority of the fluoride being used comes from China, a country that is in the dark ages as far as environmental consciousness or protection is concerned. Chinese fluoride has been shown to contain arsenic and lead.

Another thing is to always choose glass over plastic as plastic can degrade and then you are eating or drinking minute plastic particles that will wreak havoc in your body. Don't put plastic in the microwave and don't use plastic wrap in the microwave. And remember that plastic water bottles left in the heat of the car can also convert into their own little poison factories.

While food shopping, try to buy grass fed, free range beef so you are not subjected to the growth hormones and antibiotics pumped into livestock. Those supplements can have horrendous ramifications for our health. Go for wild-caught salmon versus the farmed salmon as the farmed salmon contain higher levels of toxins, including dioxin, than wild fish. The farmed fish also swim in filth due to the crowding of so many fish in one area with no outlet for their waste.

When you decide to paint around the house, look for low VOC paint, so you won't be breathing toxins for several months after the paint job. Most retailers carry a low VOC line.

Around my home, I use limited cleaning products. I buy huge bottles of white vinegar at the bulk stores and use it for everything. I also use baking soda and hydrogen peroxide, usually for stain removal. I have used the ceramic discs for washing laundry instead of laundry soap and they worked great. I don't use pesticides. I try to escort unwanted bugs out of the house by gathering them up in a tissue or newspaper or on my finger. If that fails or if they are on my most wanted list, like a cockroach or scorpion, a shoe will do. Although I do feel remorse, I apologize and send them light to join their group energy. I turn a blind eye to small ants unless there are hordes of them. After all, we have to live in harmony with nature as much as possible. And instead of using fertilizers, I stop in at Starbucks and see if they have any bagged up coffee grounds to spread around the yard. My next big project will be buying one of those big spinning composters, to cut down on garbage and create awesome nutrients for the garden. I can't wait.

9

Mercury

That quicksilver element called mercury is one of the most lethal substances on the planet. It should also be one of the most feared. It's so bad it deserves a chapter all its own.

I remember one afternoon when I was small and my little sister was sick. My mother had come in our room and put the thermometer in my sister's mouth and left us alone. As kids do, we were fooling around and the thermometer fell out of my sister's mouth onto the floor and the tip broke off sending tiny little silver balls rolling all over the floor. We were terrified of getting into trouble, so I picked up the now broken and empty thermometer and put it back into my sister's mouth, like my mother wouldn't notice. When she came back and took the thermometer out of my sister's mouth and saw that it was broken, she went psycho and started screaming. I tried to make things better by telling her that my sister had bitten off the end of the thermometer by accident. We thought it sounded better than letting it fall on the floor and break. Well, then she started screaming even more that my sister had ingested mercury and would be poisoned and die. Then we told her the truth and at least she stopped screaming. I remember picking up all those small balls of mercury with my fingers and throwing them in the garbage. Just think. We should have had a hazmat team come in. Think of that mercury in the garbage. But that was a long time ago. It seems funny now, but it could have been very serious. Thank goodness for digital thermometers.

Today mercury menaces the planet in so many ways. It is released into the atmosphere through the process of making chlorine, from improper waste handling and more importantly, from the burning of coal. Then wind, rain and snow carry it around the planet and a large amount of it gets deposited into the oceans.

Our nervous system, brain, heart, kidneys, lungs and immune system can all be affected by mercury. We can breathe mercury in from the air and ingest it through drinking water or eating seafood, especially fish. Big fish are the problem. If we eat a small fish that has a bit of mercury, it is not that serious, but as one fish eats another fish and then gets eaten and then that fish gets eaten, by the time you get to the really large fish, that's a lot of accumulated mercury. Although I really like tuna, I try to serve it at home only sporadically. It is so sad that humanity, as steward of the planet has done such a poor job and created such serious consequences.

Another form of mercury comes in the form of amalgams in dental work. If you have mercury fillings in your mouth, do yourself a favor and get them removed. I no longer have any amalgams in my mouth. All my fillings have been replaced by resin fillings. By having the mercury amalgams in your mouth, you run the risk of mercury leaching into your system over a long term basis and causing health problems. I know dental work is sky high, so do what you can, when you can.

My brother-in-law has been a dentist for almost 25 years and has been diagnosed with fibromyalgia. He has constant pain, the inability to sleep and is quite debilitated. His years of working with mercury have been implicated in the development of the illness. Don't be fearful, be aware. Knowledge is power.

10

Sweet!

Another little doozy is sweetener. We all know that refined sugar is not good for us as it's high in calories and has almost zero nutritional value. Where the danger really lies, though, is in the diet sugars. Whenever man starts messing around in the laboratory, chances are that the result will be something toxic. And that includes many of the prescription medicines churned out by the big drug companies. Who can deny that they have heard a litany of horrendous side effects being recited on television commercials about new drugs? I often think that the possible side effects, like hallucinations, blindness and stroke, sound worse than the original illness.

Whatever you do, for God's sakes, don't eat or drink anything that contains aspartame. Aspartame is better known as the brands NutraSweet, Equal, Spoonful and Equal-Measure and is embroiled in both political and medical controversies. I have read so much about the serious health risks of aspartame, that I will not touch it. I check ingredient labels like mad and would rather be fat than dead. I used to live on diet cola. I would drink it at my desk for breakfast and all throughout the day, cans and cans. Now I know that it just isn't worth it. I totally ignore any diet products because I know they will contain aspartame. And of course, any damage isn't instantaneous, it's cumulative, but do you really want to add more chemicals to the already heavy body burden?

Aspartame is a neurotoxin. It is made up of three chemicals: aspartic acid, phenylalanine and methanol. When the brain has high levels of these substances, neural cell damage occurs in the brain. This damage can cause a host of symptoms such as headaches/migraines, nausea, fatigue, depression and contribute to many severe illnesses. There is information out there that says how safe aspartame is, but I just don't buy it. Do the work, do some online research and you will have no doubts after you read the history of FDA approval which was granted in 1974. The next year an FDA task force questioned some of Searle, the manufacturer's research, and approval was revoked in 1975. Searle pushed for re-approval in 1980 which was denied due to research results indicating that the research animals developed a high incidence of brain tumors. Then, surprise, surprise, approval was granted a year later and the rest is diet soda history. Lawsuits concerning aspartame poisoning are rampant and people need to connect the dots and ask why they feel so bad.

There are some great substitutes for sugar and the diet sweeteners. Stevia is an herb which is super sweet and has virtually no calories. It has almost no effect on blood sugar.

Japan has used it as a sweetener for decades. In 1991, an anonymous complaint to the FDA about product safety, resulted in the ban of importation of stevia. Stevia consumers and importers were convinced that the FDA gave in to sugar industry pressure. The FDA approved stevia as a dietary supplement in 1995. Funnily enough, Coca Cola has developed Truvia, a stevia-derivative sweetener, and Pepsi has developed one of their own. I guess they saw the writing on the wall.

Another excellent sugar substitute is xylitol. It has many sources, but it is mainly derived from birch bark, with Denmark being the largest current producer. Xylitol looks like sugar and tastes like sugar, but it has fewer calories and does not affect the glycemic index. It promotes dental health and prevents cavities, clears up sinus and respiratory infections and helps control candida. It really is amazing. It is also pricey and hard to find. You can find it at Vitamin Shoppe, www.vitaminshoppe.com.

The last natural sweetener I'll mention is agave nectar, taken from the same agave plants used to produce tequila. It is another alternative that has a lower glycemic index. The syrup is actually sweeter than honey. It contains calcium, iron, enzymes and vitamins. One of the good things about it is that you can use it in cold drinks as it liquefies easily. Mother Nature has given us some good alternatives. Give them a try.

11

The Right Stuff

Now that we have covered what not to put into your body, there are a few things which can make a huge difference in how you feel and actually assist you in strengthening your energy field.

Wheat grass juice is one of those. It is almost like drinking pure energy. It is sprouted and grown from wheat berries, and then the young seedlings are put into a special extractor to get the juice. It is not usually something you want to do at home unless you want to buy a special setup to grow the wheat grass and an extractor. You can usually get it at a Whole Foods juice bar or a health food restaurant or store. It contains chlorophyll, amino acids, minerals, vitamins and enzymes. It heals, detoxifies and fortifies the body. It must be used quickly after juicing and you drink it like a shot or you can add it to a smoothie. It tastes really green. You drink only an ounce at a time because it is so potent.

In my mom's last months I had wheat grass juice delivered refrigerated to the house. It was a four-day supply in a small bottle. I would add a shot of wheat grass juice to some orange juice and give it to my mom like that. It was really amazing. My mom had a funky fungus toenail for years that I thought was a lost cause, but with the oxygenation of the bloodstream with the wheatgrass juice, that toenail cleared up bit by bit.

Dried wheatgrass powder will do as an alternative if you don't have access to the juice. Any other kind of green grass powder, like barley and alfalfa, is also highly beneficial. Healthy combinations with powdered grasses, herbs, fruits and vegetables among other ingredients will help if you don't have time for super healthy eating. Mix a little powder with juice in the morning and you are good to go. Liquid chlorophyll is a great way to stimulate your lymphatic system and release liquid your body may be retaining. You buy a bottle of the liquid and mix a small amount with water once a day to aid detoxification.

Apart from eating natural or organic fruits and vegetables, you can juice them or blend them. I have a Vitamix blender that you see on tv. I have used it for 10 years now and I used it to whip up a 'bomb' for my mom in the morning. I would put a bit of whatever was in the fridge into her morning shake. I used frozen blueberries, apple, melon, pineapple, carrot, beet, broccoli, ice and some orange juice and I would grind a tablespoon or two of flax seed and blend it all together. It was really delicious and loaded with fiber, vitamins, minerals, enzymes and prana. Prana is the life force of the universe and you get it through raw food. The energy is especially present in any kind of sprouts. You might want to read about raw food and maybe try a recipe once in a while or go to a raw food restaurant. Raw food chefs have taken raw food to incredible heights, creating fabulous dishes that are delicious. Just make sure that you are eating a rainbow diet – one that includes all the colors of fruits and vegetable, like red, orange, yellow, green and purple.

Keep in mind that several fruits and vegetables have sky-high amounts of pesticides. The latest report of the Environmental Working Group lists apples as having the most pesticides. After that comes celery, strawberries, peaches, spinach, imported nectarines, imported grapes, sweet bell peppers, potatoes, domestic blueberries, lettuce and kale/collard greens. Those high levels are found even after the fruit has been washed and peeled. I always buy a special spray wash in the supermarket produce section that is supposed to help remove pesticides.

The good news is that there are many fruits and vegetable that show only negligible pesticide content. The safer choices are watermelons, avocadoes, pineapples, domestic cantaloupes, mangoes, eggplants, grapefruit, mushrooms, onions and cabbage. Other countries tend to have very different standards regarding pesticide use or are not as closely regulated as the United States.

Try to cut down on meat and be aware that processed meats like bacon, breakfast sausage, hot dogs, ham, corned beef and lunchmeat contain nitrites. Nitrites can be converted to nitrosamines in the stomach. Nitrosamines can cause cancer, reduced lung function and brain tumors in children. It is possible to find nitrite-free meats, so look for them in your grocery store. If you can't find them, ask the store manager. I am sure they will be happy to accommodate you and order some and you will be creating a positive change.

Be aware that dairy products cause mucous – lots of it and can contribute to sinus infections, respiratory problems and asthma. I adore ice cream, but try not to have it anywhere in the vicinity. I can put away a pint without a problem, but later my body feels really, really bad. I have a friend who has just started a business making dairy-free ice cream. I thought dairy-free ice cream? I don't think so. But I was really surprised. She uses coconut oil which has now been found to have surprising health benefits. I tasted her chocolate mint and chai ice creams and was really surprised at how good they tasted and how healthy they are. Another factor with dairy products is that almost all cows are given hormones for rapid growth and we are now seeing children go through puberty much earlier, sometimes years earlier, than before. It is attributed to the hormones in the milk stimulating children's endocrine systems. Look for hormone-free milk. Try some almond or soy milk. There are even cheeses made from soy that are really good. I don't expect anyone to totally give up milk, cheese and ice cream. Just be aware.

There are now a lot of foods that have suddenly become popular due to their antioxidant properties. One of these is pomegranate which has been a staple in India's ayurvedic system of medicine for thousands of years. It has been used as a tonic for the heart and throat. In early clinical trials, pomegranates have been shown to help heart disease. They contain vitamin C, potassium, and tannins that scavenge free radicals. You can easily find pomegranate juice in grocery stores. Just make sure that they do not have any added artificial color or flavor.

David Wolfe, www.davidwolfe.com, author of Superfoods, is one of the foremost experts on nutrition and longevity. He recommends goji berries, reishi mushrooms, cacao, spirulina, aloe vera and coconut water/oil, among other phytoceuticals. On his website www.sacredchocolate.com, you can download a free ebook on raw chocolate. According to Wolfe, raw chocolate is one of the most nutritional foods on the planet. Who knew? On a teleseminar, Wolfe said coconut water is an excellent remedy to rejuvenate health, especially for elderly people. I often brought home fresh coconut water for my mom, from the stand where the proprietor used a machete to open the coconut and then poured the refreshing liquid in a plastic bag.

Donna Gates, author of The Body Ecology Diet and leading authority on candida, stresses the importance of including probiotics – live culture – once a day for enhanced health. She recommends kefir, a fermented milk drink. She credits a probiotic diet with healing diverse health issues, www.bodyecology.com.

If you don't think you are getting enough vitamins through your diet, you can always add the ever important vitamin C, along with vitamin E, a B complex and coenzyme Q10. Keep in mind that an alkaline diet provides great health benefits including higher energy levels.

If you are going through the Pause that refreshes, bio-identical hormone therapy is definitely healthier than hormone replacement therapy which has now been found to present many health risks. If your gynecologist doesn't know about bio-identical therapy, look until you find one that does.

I left my gynecologist because he was from the dark ages. I knew more about alternative therapies for women than he did. He knew nothing and was not interested in learning. He said he didn't have time and was too tired – he was my age! Bye, bye. I researched and found my own options. When my menstrual cycle seemed to be headed for the big round-up in the sky, I started taking herbal capsules that were a synergistic combination of dong quai, chasteberry, black cohosh and soy.

Once I had been taking them for a while, I had no menopausal symptoms at all. I know everyone is different and some women have really crippling menopausal effects, but I do know that diet and exercise can also make a difference. A really excellent supplement is maca. It is a South American plant from the radish family and the root is the portion of the plant that is used. It is an adaptogen which contains over 55 phytochemicals. It increases stamina and will regulate the body's hormone levels. If levels are too high, it will bring them down, and if levels are two low, it will bring them up. I have used maca for a long time as part of my supplements. I would suggest some reading and research which may save you many sleepless and sweaty nights in the future.

And let's not forget the guys. Research indicates that if men start taking saw palmetto, an herbal supplement, when they are forty years old, that they will avoid an enlarged prostate, frequent nighttime urination and possible prostate cancer.

It is also helpful to research other conditions you may be diagnosed with, as herbs may be extremely helpful in the healing process. Remember, they come from God's medicine chest. If your physician pooh-poohs them, find a doctor who is open-minded and includes alternative methods in his/her practice. Remember, the real power is in your hands.

12

The Tooth Museum

Disease can develop in your body in so many hidden ways. One of those ways is through root canals. Though widely hailed and accepted in mainstream dental practice, alternative dental practitioners know that it is impossible to clean every molecule of bacteria from the root of a tooth undergoing an endodoncy and that sooner or later there will be a complication. Research has shown that the bacteria that will siphon off that root canal into the body via the bloodstream will be drawn to that particular body's weakest area where it will build up and damage organs over a period of many years.

In some people that might be the heart, causing heart disease. In others it may be the kidneys, leading to kidney disease. Research has shown that when the root canal is pulled and a cavitation done – a scraping of the bone - the heart disease or kidney disease disappears. If you say this to a mainstream dentist, you most likely will be laughed right out of the office.

Dr. Jose Luis Romo has been my doctor for 28 years. Originally an allopathic physician, over the years he has studied alternative medicine and now rarely uses traditional medical practices, as he finds that the body can heal itself just fine when given natural support. Dr. Romo uses acupuncture, colonics, magnet therapy, ozone therapy, homeopathy, chelation therapy and cellular anti-aging. He studied biological dentistry in Germany, where they teach that every tooth is connected to an organ or specific area in the body and that the health of that tooth affects the health of that organ or area. Over the years he has shown me many different teeth and recounted the stories behind them, what I call, The Tooth Museum.

Jose always shows me the offending tooth in a small clear, plastic case. It is hard to believe that such a small thing could have caused so much havoc in the body. In one instance, Jose had been telling a patient for almost twenty years that his chronic back pain was caused by the root canal in his mouth. The patient absolutely refused to accept that diagnosis until one day, when he could stand the pain no more. He finally had the tooth removed, and his back pain disappeared.

In another case, a woman had been trying to become pregnant for fourteen years. She went to numerous specialists and tried many different treatments to assist her fertility. When she went to Dr. Romo, he sent her for a panoramic mouth x-ray. He discovered that one of her teeth had a tumor on the tip of its root. He advised her to get the tooth removed. She removed the tooth and became pregnant within one month.

One day Jose was called by the manager of a hotel, who explained that one of his staff had incredible abdominal pain and was due to be operated on for exploratory surgery the next day. The patient was examined, but nothing showed up. He had lab tests and an ultrasound and still nothing showed up. Jose looked in the man's mouth and found a cavernous cavity in one of the man's teeth. The patient had not had pain because the tooth had a root canal. Even with the root canal, bacteria from the decaying tooth was passing into the bloodstream and body. The tooth was extracted later that day and the abdominal pain was gone.

I have had all my root canals pulled. You can have bridgework done to compensate for the missing tooth or you can have a removable tooth made to fill the space. It holds onto your gums with small wings. If you have a lot of root canals, you are probably dizzy with all the dollar signs in front of your eyes right now. Remember, little by little. I know from experience that there are really gifted dentists in Mexico that charge only a fraction of what is paid for the same services in the states.

I have read about people going to other countries as well. If you are interested, do a little research. Let Google do the work. If you don't have a computer, go to a cyber cafe or the local public library. If you don't know how to use the internet, ask someone to show you how to click on 'Launch Internet' and then ask them to show you how to type the address of Google in the appropriate space and then how to enter your search topic. You will not believe how easy it is and how much information you will have access to. All change starts with one small step.

13

Everything Comes Out In the End

A lot has been written about colonics – intestinal cleansing with water – which is usually the medical community saying how dangerous and unnecessary they are. I beg to differ. I have been doing my own colonics for about 22 years now. I have had two colonoscopies clean as a whistle, which I attribute in large part to the care I have given my colon over the years.

I know that doctors say that the colon cleans itself, but I have found that to be not quite accurate. The colon is about five feet long and normally cleanses itself by moving waste along with peristaltic motion. When you eat heavy-duty junk food that has no fiber and don't drink enough water, it is easy for everything to just sit there for a long time before the waste moves on. Think of leftover pizza the next morning. Have you ever touched the cheese and felt how hard it is?

Now, just think that every time you have a situation like that, that a little tiny bit of waste, like the hard cheese, gets stuck in the curvy walls of the colon. Little by little over years of poor eating habits, it's like plastering those walls with mucous and food particles. The walls need to be clear as they assist in the digestive process. Finally, your colon seems clean and everything keeps moving, but in reality there is all this old, putrefied matter built up in your colon, creating a toxic situation and hampering the body's ability to absorb nutrition.

I remember reading a book about colon cleansing, where the author recounted how 28 years earlier she had traveled to a part of the country where a certain berry grew. It was the only place where that particular berry grew. All those years later, when she was doing a colon cleansing, one of those berries came out during the process. That berry had been in her colon for 28 years, impacted with fecal matter in the lining of her colon! No, it isn't pretty, but it's true.

When I did my first colon cleansing ever, I took herbs specially formulated for the cleansing and did my own colonics. Now the next part is something that my daughter would consider 'too much information' so you can skip ahead if you would like. But I would check out what was coming out from the cleanse. Weird-looking stuff came out, things that looked alien for want of a better description. Some of it looked exactly like it had been stuck on the wall of my colon a long time, because it had the same shape as you would imagine that your colon has, and it was about ten inches long. I just had to, yes, touch it and it felt like plastic, that hard. I know, really gross. So there was no doubt in my mind after that about the importance of colon cleansing, and colonics in particular. I am a skeptic by nature and really have to see proof before I get on the bandwagon.

When you go for colonic therapy, normally it is done with an instrument that allows the water to flow into your rectum and colon and at the same time allows the wastewater to leave. My own personal colonic equipment is more simple, with a colonic board, a hose and a small tube. Doctors always say that there is a chance of rectal perforation with a colonic. Anyone performing a colonic is super gentle through the process. Trust me, the only way I could possibly perforate anything would be if an earthquake happened at the exact moment that I was inserting the tube!

Many products are on the market for detox and colon cleanse. I have used products from www.ariseandshine.com with great success. Always check with your healthcare professional before you start any cleanse. Your body is a temple that houses the spectacular light of the Creator. The cleaner your body and energy field, the more light you can embody, assisting both personal and planetary transformation.

14

The Hip Bone's Connected to the Thigh Bone

The free flow of energy in the body is so important right now for the quantum leap we are undergoing. One way to keep the energy moving is through chiropractic care. Energy from the nervous system flows through the spine and out into the body via the nerves. When we experience stress, bad diet or tax our body with heavy lifting or a fall, our spine goes out of alignment causing pain, immune deficiency and a host of other problems. This is called a subluxation. Chiropractors are trained to adjust the spine so it is properly aligned and that the energy flows freely into the rest of the body.

When I have had tremendous pain of the back, neck or shoulders, I have gone to my chiropractor who adjusts my body and I am well by the next day. Every once in a while when I trip and fall or take a spill from my bike, I immediately go to the chiropractor so the injury can be addressed before it has time to settle into my body. My chiropractor, Basil, told me about one of his patients, a woman whose father had been a chiropractor. She had received chiropractic care since she was a child and had carried it on throughout her life. She was youthful, active and full of vitality into her late eighties and owed it to chiropractic care.

When my daughter was a newborn, she had really bad constipation. Nothing we did seemed to make a difference. I had a natural childbirth with her, pushing for three hours. Alyssa was a nine pound baby and childbirth was rough for both of us. One day when I was at the chiropractor's for an adjustment, I mentioned in conversation about my daughter's problem. He took a look at her and said that her atlas was out, probably due to the strenuous childbirth. He gave her a small adjustment and she was never constipated again. He said babies were the easiest to adjust as they were the closest to God's blueprint, having just been born.

If you have a serious problem, you will probably need several adjustments to recover balance and alignment in your body. Most of the time, one adjustment will do and you only need go back for a tune-up a few times a year.

Acupuncture also frees up energy in the body. Chinese medicine has been used for about 3,000 years. They believe that energy meridians run through the body and that when these meridians are blocked due to stress and illness, the body is unable to heal itself. By placing the acupuncture needles at the proper points, the blockages are opened, restoring energy flow.

At a particularly stressful time in my life, I developed severe pain in my sciatic nerve and I could not lift my leg to put on a pair of pants. I saw Dr. Romo and he got me started on daily acupuncture. In less than 10 days I was fine, with some relief beginning immediately. When I was pregnant, my husband had Bell's palsy with half his face paralyzed. Once again Dr.Romo used facial acupuncture and within two weeks the paralysis was gone.

When my mom first came to live with me, she was over-medicated and in really poor health. She could hardly walk and when she got into the car I needed to pick her leg up by her pant leg in order to get it into the car. She was eighty years old. After about six months of treatment with Dr. Romo involving dietary changes, less meds and twice weekly acupuncture, my mom regained her ability to walk and was able to go shopping for her groceries. She began to paint again after having lost the ability several years before.

People always think that acupuncture is painful – like being a human pin cushion. But you barely feel it. Dr. Romo uses electricity with his acupuncture, connecting wires which send a small current through the needle. This method increases the effectiveness of the acupuncture. Keep the energy flowing through your body and other changes will come much easier.

15

Wired

EMFs or electromagnetic frequencies fill the air around us. They are unseen, but not unfelt. If we are not maintaining a high vibratory state, they affect our energy field and can cause debilitating illness affecting the hypothalamus and cortex of the brain. Our energy field is electromagnetic in nature and grounds our body to the Schumann Resonance, the electromagnetic waves surrounding our planet. The Schumann Resonance is like the earth's heartbeat. There are about 1,000 electrical storms around the planet at any given time, with about 200 lightening strikes a minute which maintain the energy field in our atmosphere. The Schumann Resonance was 7.8 for many centuries, but recently has begun to speed up to 12, creating a quickening, part of the energy shift we are experiencing.

It is quite overwhelming when we think of all the EMF energy that is present in our homes with microwaves, refrigerators, televisions, computers and phones. Wi-Fi generates a powerful microwave energy field throughout the home. Research shows that the energy affects the ions in the cells that regulate metabolism, knocking out lithium, potassium and calcium from the cells, all vital to our body's functions. In Europe, microwave energy has been implicated in causing attention deficit syndrome in children, by damaging their vulnerable developing brains and nervous systems. It is documented that people living near cell phone towers have problems sleeping as the energy prevents the body from relaxing.

Recently, I listened to an interview with inventor and scientist Jean Gallick. For 20 years she experienced a range of serious health problems that would not be cured. She went from specialist to specialist and tried many healing modalities, but had no relief until she discovered she was highly sensitive to electromagnetic energy, which was the source of her arthritis, asthma and headaches. She researched until she created a line of products to shield the body and home from harmful electromagnetic energy. Her products can be found at www.earthcalm.com. There are pendants to be worn around the neck, small discs to stick on a cell phone and plug-in devices which create a grounding field in the home.

Several years ago I did an experiment to see if a cell phone disc from another company really worked. Dr. Romo has a computer hooked up to sensors that you hold in your hands while he stimulates points on the fingertips. The computer gives a read-out of the body's health, with detailed information about many organs and systems. I asked him to help me with the experiment. First I had him test me to give a base for comparison. Then I put my cell phone to my ear and they called me and conducted the computer test once again while I stayed on the phone. My readings plummeted while I was on the phone.

Then I stuck the shield chip onto my cell phone and had them test me again. My readings went up, but they did not reach the values of my first reading. It was clear, though, that the cell phone shield had aided in reducing the effect from the radiation coming from the phone.

For years science has said that there is no proven danger from the microwaves from cell phones. Well, just last week I heard on the news that research is indicating that there is a very real danger from holding cell phones next to your brain. Once again this is something to be aware of and decide if you want to take action or not.

16

That Magnetic Attraction

If you research magnetic therapy, like so many alternate healing methods, you will find that there is no explanation for how it works. In fact, you will see that some scientists state emphatically that it doesn't work, that it's a hoax. I can only go by my personal experience and say that it does, indeed work and that it has helped my family and friends with many different health issues.

While my mom was bedridden, she would develop bedsores from time to time and quite frequently, aches and pains in her hips, legs and other parts of her body. I had learned about magnetic therapy from Dr. Romo who had taken courses with an eighty-year-old magnet master and started using it in his practice. I was blessed to have a supply of magnets to help my mom's discomfort. When she complained of pain, I would tape small magnets on the distressed area and in a few days, sometimes in a day, she would no longer have pain. I would put larger magnets under a bedsore and it would heal quickly.

When I injure myself, I immediately tape on magnets to start the healing process. Last week I had really bad pain in my wrist. I taped the small magnets on the most painful points, and by the next day my wrist was much better. Some researchers think that the magnets stimulate blood circulation which then stimulates the cells to regenerate. I don't need to know how it works, I only know that it does work and I don't hesitate to use it. When my daughter injures herself during sports, I use magnets for the injury.

My friend, Imperia, was the protégé of the same magnet master that Dr. Romo studied with. She does incredible diagnostic work with kiniesiology muscle testing, and then treats whatever imbalance she finds. When my sister was visiting, I took her to see Imperia and it was amazing that Imperia could pinpoint so many health issues that my sister had at the time. Then Imperia put magnets on all the organs and areas indicated in her diagnostic testing. The basis for the healing is that we all have a lot of virus, bacteria and parasites in our bodies which are responsible for many of our health problems. Imperia's teacher believes the magnetic therapy unravels and destroys the genetic material of the opportunistic organisms, which prevents them from reproducing and ultimately kills them. Imperia had a patient who was HIV positive. She treated him for several months. When he went back to the doctor to check his status, the doctor found no trace of the virus. I had a friend several years ago who told me the same thing. He has been diagnosed as

HIV positive, but after several weeks of magnet therapy by a different healer, he no longer had the virus. I know that there are probably people reading this that say they don't believe it, but I respect Imperia's integrity without question.

When Imperia did a diagnostic session with me, one of the first things she said was that I had a shrimp intoxication in my body. I told her that it couldn't be, because I was allergic to shrimp. When I was eight-years-old, I had eaten shrimp for the first time, my body blew up twice its size with hives and I was taken to Children's Memorial Hospital in Chicago. I've never had shrimp since. Imperia told me that incident caused the diagnosis and that for 50 years my body had harbored that imbalance. She also picked up other things that had been bothering me.

I believe magnet therapy is so important, that I urge you to find a practitioner, so when you need one you will have someone you trust. That person can assist you to buy some magnets and teach you how to use them, so when you need them you will have them. I sleep on a magnetic pad because the magnets balance the energy field in the body and allow it to absorb and use more of the light that is flooding the planet. With the magnets, we are attuned to the earth's energy.

17

Sign On the Dotted Line

We all come into this lifetime with a soul contract as to what we expect to do and accomplish while we are in this dimension. Time is spent between incarnations to rest, to study or possibly to experience other dimensions before deciding exactly what we need or would like to learn while here. Part of the plan is to connect with other souls from previous lifetimes to work out karma and balance any situation which we feel was not handled with love during a particular incarnation. We also choose our parents and the circumstances we would like to be born into. Upon reflection, you may have an idea why your life has unfolded the way that it has or maybe you think you would never have chosen your life in a million years!

Free will always plays an important part of any lifetime. Although a soul may come in with a certain plan including a career and mate, the individual may choose to go a different route and totally deviate from the original contract. Many do and that is how we get caught up on the wheel of karma where it is not uncommon for a soul to have up to 800 previous lifetimes. Just think of all the people, places and experiences we carry in our DNA and it is easy to see why we are the complicated beings we are with baggage not just from this lifetime, but myriad lifetimes full of passion and emotion.

When we enter as infants, the veil comes down and we go through a forgetting of who we were before and what it is like on the other side. They say that babies have not quite lost all their perception of the other side and that they can still see entities from across the veil. I suspect that's true as I remember when my daughter was a baby and she was clearly looking up at something and laughing so delightedly that I could only reason that she was seeing someone that I couldn't. Little by little children are raised to forget the other side and chastised if they talk about a secret friend or seeing their deceased grandparent.

You are here right now because you have chosen to be here right now and have chosen to be a part of the shift in consciousness of this planet. A tremendous number of souls wanted to incarnate at this time, but preference was given to those souls who could contribute to the overall success of the planetary shift. You are here for a reason. It may not be that you need to complete a grand plan or to become a leader of men. It may be enough for you to hold space, to hold the love and light that is flooding into the planet as a beacon to not only those in your life, but those that you merely pass on the street or sit next to on the subway. The incredible force of love is so brilliant and complete that it infuses all that it comes in contact with. That is why it is so important for us to be in the moment, aware of the energy and possibilities and to keep our own energy fields at a high vibrational level. I have noticed the effect I have on someone when I feel that my energy is strong and I look that person right in the eyes. There is a visible change in that person. Did you see the movie Avatar? Do you remember when they say 'I see you?' We must really 'see' the other people with which we share this reality. Actually, we are looking at ourselves, because we are all One. We are looking in a mirror. We are looking in our own eyes.

Start right now and set a clear intention to expand your consciousness with the love flooding the planet. Sit in a comfortable position, close your eyes and breathe in deeply and slowly and then deeply exhale until you feel you have shifted into another mode. See the brilliant light which is streaming from the heart of the galaxy, passing through the sun and then onto our planet. See it coming in through your soul star, the chakra which is about fourteen inches above your head, and then flooding your body with the light. Continue to breathe deeply and slowly, circulating the light in your body. Breathe in photon energy through your soul star and then breathe it out into your surroundings. Do this for at least five minutes or as long as you'd like. Create the intention to anchor this energy into your life. Slowly open your eyes and gently return to your surroundings. And so it is.

18

Voices

During the time that I cared for my mom, I didn't get out of the house much. But I discovered teleconferences, where you could hear a variety of interviews with self-help speakers either by telephone or the internet. I have an unlimited calls phone package, so I use the phone when I can. It's more comfortable for me to lie on the bed and listen rather than sit at my computer. I was fortunate to hear so many intelligent and gifted individuals talk about their life experience and expertise. It broadened the scope of my world.

When I first began, I knew of only one teleconference series, but now there are several. All of them are run by high vibrational people who care about the planet and the vast changes and shifts we are experiencing. Usually the calls are muted when I join, but sometimes the lines are open and the interviewer will ask your name and city when you join the call. I have been amazed at the people from all the different states and sometimes Canada, Mexico and beyond who are on the call. Sometimes the call includes an energy session or meditation. I can visualize the web of light that we are creating as our energies merge around the planet.

The other day I participated in a summer solstice meditation with Marie Diamond, www.mariediamond.com. Marie does feng shui among other things. There were almost 1200 people from 180 countries on the line. The meditation was very beautiful and included those people below the equator experiencing the winter solstice in their hemisphere. I was energized for the rest of the day.

Sometimes I have participated in three conferences back-to-back and I felt like I was in school again. Last week I listened to Neale Donald Walsch, the author of Conversations with God. I have also listened to Gregg Braden, visionary scientist who authored many books, including his latest, The Spontaneous Healing of Belief. The speakers are many and the topics are varied, including alternative health, energy medicine, spirituality, nutrition, manifesting abundance and many more. Sometimes an actual energy healing is performed as there really is no time or space and the energy easily passes to everyone on the call.

Usually a schedule is posted for several months in advance, so you can plan the conferences you will attend. They are held in the early afternoon or evening. If you can't participate, they will post a 48 hour replay right after the conference. And the best part is..........they're free! If you are financially challenged right now, as long as you have access to a computer, you can participate. Even if you don't have a computer, you can interest one of your friends in the topics and you can listen together, or even in a group. I don't always resonate with the speaker or the topic, so I opt out after about ten minutes. If you had to pay these speakers for a private consultation, it would cost you lots of money. So take advantage of this great option. I feel very blessed with the conferences I have attended.

The first conferences I listened to were created by Linda Pannell who always had cutting edge speakers and topics. But with the rapid growth of the seminars, I now include the speakers listed below:

Linda Pannell, www.worldchangingwisdom.com.
Sheila Gale, www.TheSheilaShow.com,
Jennifer McLean, www.healingwiththemasters.com,
Deb Thompson, www.LivingEnergySecrets.com,
Adoley Odunton, www.wellnessrevolutionsummit.com
Darius M. Barazandeh, www.youwealthrevolution.com

They always provide a form on their webpage to submit a question before the session. I am sure once you begin to listen to the different series, you will come upon even more opportunities. Make the time to listen to the seminars. If I am tight on time, I listen to a replay while I am doing other things on the computer. They are enjoyable and they can be life changing.

19

Water, Water, Everywhere

Dr. Masuru Emoto is a Japanese researcher and author of Messages from Water. Emoto discovered that the molecular structure of water can be influenced by intention, meditation, prayer and music. His experiments centered on having people concentrate on water samples. For the positive sample, the participants would meditate on the water sample using the word gratitude or love. For the negative sample, the participants would send the energy of the words you fool. After a set time, the samples were then frozen. Later, the water's molecular structure was examined under a microscope and photos were taken.

The positive samples showed beautiful crystalline shapes similar to snowflakes, while the negative samples were misshapen, almost like cancerous growths. What inspirational results, the fact that thought can affect the molecular structure of the water and create order and beauty. How important to know that our daily meditations and prayers can assist the planet by sending love and gratitude to all bodies of water around the planet - lakes, streams, rivers and oceans. We can visualize the Gulf waters pristine and the Japanese coastal waters free from radiation. And since our bodies are 70% water, we can influence our own health. It is another reminder that our thoughts create reality and that we can better the world we live in.

I attended a lecture given by Emoto several years ago. He is an endearing man with a humble demeanor. His wife accompanied him and was very sweet. She delighted in the story that her husband wanted to publish his book when he had completed his research, but they didn't have the funds. She then surprised him with the full amount of money he needed for the publication. She had secretly been putting away money over their long marriage.

Emoto stressed how important it is that his research is taught to children around the world. He wants them to know that with love and gratitude they can change the world. His hope is to teach the children so they will create peace on earth. 'Messages from Water' has been released in a children's version and has been translated into ten languages. Emoto has already donated almost 260,000 books to children around the world. His goal is to donate a total of 650 million copies to children over the next several years. He calls this the Emoto Peace Project, www.masuru-emoto.net.

Emoto has a dreamer quality. At the end of his lecture, he put the words from John Lennon's Imagine on the auditorium screen and encouraged everyone to sing along with the music. It was very beautiful.

If only all news about water was so positive. Unfortunately, there are so many places around the world where women have to walk miles and miles to bring water for cooking and drinking. Sometimes the quality of the water is muddy and diseased, but it is their only option. Every day, hundreds of children die because of dirty drinking water. It is said that in the future, our wars will be fought over water and that right now, there are concerns jockeying for control of the world's water. Does that even surprise you? A documentary was produced on just this issue, Blue Gold: World Water Waters, and was featured on PBS. Go to the website, www.bluegold-worldwaterwars.com, to view it and for more information. Yes, we can create our reality with our thoughts, but as we live in this three dimensional world at the moment, we also need to be aware and take action where appropriate.

A man named B.J. Kjaer is doing just that. Kjaer is co-founder of SolarRain Water. He and his partners worked four years to develop a more efficient way to turn ocean water into fresh drinking water. The current method of desalination has about 50% waste in the reverse osmosis process. With SolarRain's process there is only 20% waste. Their process, like nature, evaporates and condenses the salt water converting it to pure fresh water. Over 80% of their energy is provided by evacuated solar tube technology. Solar generated thermal energy is used in the evaporative process. They provide bottled water to the San Diego area. Their process preserves the mineral balance of the water, which is akin to the mineral content in our blood. They have even found a way to lessen the impact of the plastic bottles that are used to bottle the water. A company in Arizona adds a fatty acid to the plastic which works as a catalyst for the digestion of the plastic by microbes. Instead of languishing thousands of years in landfills, the bottles can be broken down in about a year! Amazing. Although they are converting water only in San Diego at present, they hope that their process will provide valuable water for the planet in the future, www.solarrainwatery.com.

Take a moment to energize our planet's water supply. Close your eyes and breathe deeply several times until you have entered a quiet place. Now place your attention on our precious water supply. Begin by loving, thanking and sending light to the water that runs in your home. Next, expand that love and send it to the water sources around the area where you live. Continue to send the light and gratitude to the lakes, streams and rivers around the world. See them clear, clean and sparkling in brilliant sunlight. Then send the light to all our oceans and especially the hot spots of the Gulf oil spill and Japan's radiation leaks into the sea. See the cleansing process happening with the love dissolving the oil and transmuting the radioactive energy into harmless electrons. Send a final blast of gratitude, light and love to all water on the planet in the form of a blinding flash of light. Slowly open your eyes. And so it is.

Do this short meditation at least once a day. Do it with your family around the dinner table. The more people that do the meditation, the effect is exponential. Get used to using your energy for the good of all and our precious Mother Earth.

20

It's in the Stars

Astrology gets a bad rap. It is usually portrayed as something hokey, with the astrologer wearing a bandanna with big hoop earrings.

Nothing could be further from the truth. Of course, if you look at sun sign astrology that you find in newspapers and magazines, you are not looking at the complex science that astrology really is. I always wanted to have an astrology reading, but it just never crossed my path until I went to a favorite restaurant in Chicago in 1979. An astrologer was giving inexpensive flat chart readings (based on the day, though not the minute) in the bar. I had the fifteen minute reading. What she told me in fifteen minutes was nothing that I didn't already know about myself. But it so accurately characterized me and my idiosyncrasies, I wanted to know how she did that in fifteen minutes. Later that year I had a full chart reading, based on the minute I was born and the place, and the information was even more relevant.

Being the do-it-yourselfer that I am, I studied astrology with Barbara Schermer, author of Astrology Alive, www.astrologyalive.com. In those times it took about an hour to do a chart, using latitudes, longitudes and logarithms. I find it really incredible that now I just plug the information into my computer program and in seconds the chart is ready. Sun sign astrology from the newspaper is so vague because it addresses only one aspect of the astrology chart. Your chart is a blueprint of the heavens at the place and moment you were born. It locks into place not only your sun sign, but nine other planets and your ascendant and midheaven. Some astrologers will include asteroids or karmic points as well. The chart explains your personality traits and gives an idea of strengths, weaknesses, potential challenges and opportunities. Since astrology is based on planetary symbols and their interpretation, the synthesis of the information is the key to a useful reading.

Astrology is especially valuable in the timing of events. By looking at the current position of planets in relation to the planetary placement of the natal chart, it's possible to see the energy of life circumstances. For example, if someone wants to invest in a project and I see that the planet Neptune is aspecting the chart at the time, I would caution the person to go slowly and have reservations. Among other things, Neptune can signify deception by other parties, something concealed, or just not seeing the circumstances clearly. It's an oversimplification, but you get the idea. Astrology has provided valuable information throughout my life. I don't consult it on a daily basis or let it make my decisions for me, but it is like having a trusted advisor, similar to the kings of old and their advisors.

Remember Ronald Reagan and his wife's astrologer and all the ridicule it generated? Actually, it wasn't a bad idea. The United States has its own chart and so does every other country in the world. Sometimes I read scholarly astrological publications and it is really fascinating to see trends unfolding in the news which are mirrored in the US chart or those of politicians. Cayelin Castell, www.cayelincastell.com, offers Celestial Timings once a month which give a good summary of what's up astrologically.

Whenever there is a new moon or a full moon, I like to watch the world news to see what unfolds. There is much energy around the lunations, with a new moon harboring new beginnings and a full moon signaling a culmination or revelation. The sign that the lunation is in, gives a clue as to the flavor of the events and circumstances. For instance, during a recent full moon in Scorpio, a sign of reproduction and sexuality, the headlines screamed the revelation of an Arnold Schwarzenegger love child and rape charges brought against the head of the International Monetary Fund.

When I worked in travel, I would give my staff predictions about their welcome meetings for arriving tourists, based on what sign the moon was in. I could tell them if the guests would be happy, if they would be chatty, if they would be inclined to buy tours and if so, which ones. At first they thought I was nuts. Then when they saw that I could call the group mood, they would start to ask me ahead of time what their group would be like. I remember warning them that an eclipse was scheduled for a weekend filled with charter plane arrivals. It was in Libra, which signifies partnership and public relations among other things. My reps reported that a married couple had such a terrible argument that the hotel had to hide the wife in another room, and that two passengers got into a fistfight waiting in line for their flight.

Eclipses are powerful and what I call people movers. If an eclipse aspects a natal chart, usually there is something notable occurring in that person's life. The energy begins weeks before and ends weeks after. It is a process. People are born, people die. Actually an eclipse is a time when many people decide to leave this dimension. My mom died a few hours before an eclipse which was aspecting the Sun in her natal chart. Many times famous people are born or die at an eclipse. Princess Diana died at an eclipse. People also get sick, get better, get a job, lose a job, buy or sell a house, move across the country, fall in love, get divorced and on and on. So it is beneficial to be aware of eclipses and if they are aspecting your chart so you can be heads up about the energy and how it figures in your life. If the eclipse is not aspecting your chart, you need to be aware that energy is high and to be extra cautious driving and to avoid anyone showing erratic behavior. Low vibrational people are susceptible to the strong energy and may act out without even knowing why. Sometimes long hidden information surfaces around an eclipse, like the recent arrest of a mobster on the most wanted list for sixteen years.

One of the most fascinating astrological cycles, though, is the Saturn return. The planet Saturn returns to its natal position every 28 to 29 years, meaning that when we are around 28 and then 58, we experience the energy of Saturn on our natal chart. It deals out just merits, with rewards or lessons, over a two-year period. If you have been doing what you should be doing for the years prior to your return, you will likely have a positive growth experience. If you haven't been on a positive path in the previous years, Saturn may give you a cosmic kick in the butt to get you back on track with your original life purpose. I find it interesting to read online or in a magazine about people and note things that happen to them at age 28 and 58. People can become famous, go through health challenges and almost anything else that you can imagine. When I see someone has died at those ages, I know it is because they have completed their mission here and that it is time to return home. I have seen stars become famous at their first Saturn return and then fall into obscurity until their second Saturn return when they are rediscovered. A perfect example of that is Betty White. She is going through her third Saturn return at 88 years. She has had a revival and has been in tv commercials, she has a tv show, she was in a movie, on Saturday Night Live and on talk shows. Most people do not get to their third Saturn return. Just recently I called a friend I hadn't talked to in about two years. I have his astrology chart from 30 years ago and saw that he was going through his second Saturn return. I called and asked what was going on in his life. He is an archeologist and had just published three books and is now experiencing a degree of recognition.

Astrology can definitely be an aid in guiding you to your life purpose and assisting you to recognize the dynamics in any situation you experience. It is a tool and should never be used to make your decisions for you. There are astrologers in your community who will help you maximize use of the energy flooding the planet now, in line with your given blueprint. And they don't wear bandannas.

21

You have a choice Neo...

Morpheus – The Matrix I

Did you see The Matrix? Well even if you didn't, Neo has to decide whether he takes the blue pill and wakes to his normal life, or he takes the red pill and learns the truth. Well, life is asking you that very thing right now. What will you do? Although the following information is controversial, I have studied the topics for over three decades and do not doubt their truth. Feel free to do your own research. You'll be surprised.

Are there things that have been hidden from the human race for eons? Yes.

Do aliens exist? Yes.

Are there huge conglomerates manipulating the world's money and politics from behind the scenes? Yes.

Is the media controlled as to what content they allow you to see? Yes.

Do they want us to remain numb and unaware and so preoccupied with day-to-day survival that we blindly believe whatever they throw at us? Yes.

Is HAARP being used for weather control and quite possibly earth movements? Yes.

Are worldwide governments preparing underground areas to flee in the worst case scenario? Yes.

Do chem trails exist? Yes.

Have many of the lethal viruses been created in a laboratory? Yes.

Does it matter? No. For centuries mankind has been manipulated by powerful interests who care about only two things, money and power. If man has flourished and created art and developed science, it is in spite of the powers that be controlling all facets of our existence. When we are in a state of fear, our chakras close down and we are unable to utilize the powerful energy streaming into the planet. If we are afraid of foreclosure, afraid of disease, afraid of hurricanes, tornadoes and earthquakes and afraid of a chaotic society, we are unable to center and create our own reality. Those in control know this. They know about energy and the transformation that the planet is entering right now. The government has known about these things for decades. Listen to the now famous speech of President Dwight D. Eisenhower where he cautions us about the military and industrial complex as he was leaving office.

We are not talking about a dark cabal. We are talking about the executive of Tyco who had a $6,000 shower curtain and others like him. We are talking about individuals who have lost their humanity and replaced it with greed. We are talking about companies who purchase a country's most valuable assets, and then enslave its citizens to work for penny wages. We are talking about the financial institutions that created the reprehensible foreclosure fiasco and caused our country to teeter on the brink of financial disaster.

But what they don't know is that no matter how diligently they try to hang on to the status quo, that change is inevitable and that the light streaming into the planet is a tremendous force. We can forge a new world of equality and incredible beauty. We can ensure that every person has food, clean water and an education. We can begin to repair the damage that has wantonly been visited upon the planet with strip mining, chemical use, oil drilling, industrial pollution and other irresponsible practices.

Wake up and smell the coffee. Be discerning. Don't believe everything you read, see online or watch on tv. Keep your energy flowing and focus on positive change. Whatever you do, do not go into fear because you cannot create from a place of fear. Know that the photon energy is incredibly powerful and as long as we focus on the change we want, we can influence every area of our lives.

None of the millennia of history matters now. All that matters is this moment. All that matters is high, clear intent of the love in our hearts connected with the love streaming from the heart of our galaxy. Each and every one of us matters. Together we are a force of crystalline light embracing the earth.

22

Wipe That Smile on Your Face

The chapter title is from a Buick ad that I saw in a magazine. I saved it to put on the wall in my studio. I adore magazines and love to cut things out and save them. I have folders with travel information, recipes, interesting stories, health and on and on. I suppose when I die, that whoever looks through my things will not even open a folder. They'll probably just say throw all that junk in the garbage. But for now, they are my treasures. In high school they had us make joy books. We cut out things from magazines and gathered or wrote poetry and put together beautiful books to gift to a friend to celebrate them or to bring joy to their life. But I digress.

A smile is such a universal expression, doesn't cost anything and can accomplish so much in just a moment. I have noticed people that look really mad, grouchy or even scary, but when you smile at them, their faces just melt in the most beautiful way. If you walk around with a smile on your face you feel happy. I have been following my own advice and experimenting with this and it really works. Plus, it really changes people's energy in the most delightful way. Now I know you are probably thinking, well I don't need anybody telling me to smile, I can figure out that for myself. Right. But maybe you need someone to remind you to do it. We all race around with so many things on our mind, and places to go and problems to solve and sometimes with great sorrow in our heart. We don't even notice what kind of expression we have on our face. Be mindful, try smiling a lot more often. It is such an easy and fun way to raise our vibrational level.

In Robert Holden's book, Living Wonderfully, he recounts his research findings where children smiled between 300 and 400 times a day, and they laughed about 150 times a day. Adults laugh about 15 times a day. Ouch. Dr. Madan Kataria, a cardiologist in India, has a remedy for that. He is founder of Laughter Yoga www.laughteryogaamerica.com that reaches out to 60 countries in the world. Sign up for their newsletter and you get lots of freebies. Laughter Yoga consists of yogic breathing and stretches with deliberate laughing. When people laugh, highly beneficial oxygenation takes place. Nobel Prize winner Dr. Otto Warburg found that cancer develops when there is a low level of oxygen in the cells. Laughter strengthens the immune system, releases feel-good endorphins, exercises the body and massages internal organs. Great stuff from a belly laugh! Neuroscientists at Stanford University put together the funniest jokes they could find and asked test participants to read them while they were in an MRI machine. Results showed that the part of the brain stimulated by the laughter was the same part of the brain that is stimulated by drugs, sexual attraction and money.

Dr. Kataria has started 3,000 Laughter Clubs around India with a goal to open one million clubs around the world. His Laughter Yoga is used in prisons where it helps reduce anger and violence, creates cooperation and reduces illness. When used with senior citizens, it alleviates depression, and they have better health and mobility. It is also used in rehabilitation, cancer centers and homeless shelters. Many people credit the Laughter Yoga with curing their cancer. One woman said she holds her electric bill in front of her and laughs and laughs until her stress about the high bill is gone. Just imagine if everyone around the world started doing Laughter Yoga. Remember that we manifest from a place of joy and gratitude. Adding thankfulness to the joyous laughter would create an explosive high vibration, allowing us to anchor positive change on a global scale. What a fun way to change the world.

Consult the website for more information on the Laughter Yoga and then start your own club with friends and family. You have nothing to lose and everything to gain. Some of the best times I remember in my life are where I was laughing so hard that tears rolled down my cheek. How delicious.

23

Even a small star shines in the darkness.

Finnish proverb

There is a reason you are reading this book. You are a Lightworker. You have chosen to be on this planet at this time to use your light and love to assist humanity with this great evolutionary step to love and compassion. Whether you are here to create great change or to hold the light and carry it through daily life, you are here to participate. And there are so many ways you can do it, starting with the simplest idea.

Everyone knows it's better to give than receive, but it is not as widely known that the act of giving releases serotonin, a feel-good neurotransmitter in the brain of the person that is giving. Serotonin is also released in the brain of the person who receives and in the brain of anyone witnessing the act. So apart from being the right thing to do, kindness and generosity make us feel good. If we make it a daily practice to perform random acts of kindness and giving, our vibrational level will shoot up, we will manifest faster and easier and the world will be a far better place.

In her book 29 Gifts: How a Month of Giving Can Change Your Life, Cami Walker describes her descent into desperation after her diagnosis of multiple sclerosis shortly after she married. A wise medicine woman from South Africa told her she was too focused on herself and gave her the prescription to give away 29 gifts in 29 days. She balked at first at the silly concept until she tried it months later, and recounts the tremendous shift it created in her life. Her gifts were not always material, but also of time, compassion or support. She has continued to start another 29 days every time she finishes a cycle. Cami has a website, www.29Gifts.org, with almost 15,000 members in 43 countries who want to change the world one gift at a time. Why don't you take the 29 day challenge?

Some ideas have grown exponentially until they become a wave of change. Muhammad Yunus created such a wave with a simple idea. The Nobel Peace Prize winner decided it would be a good idea to lend money to poor people, to the very people usually excluded by banks. He began by lending $27 to 42 bamboo weavers in his home country of Bangladesh. The weavers prospered, repaid the loan and laid way for Yunus to found Grameen Bank and the practice of microlending. Since 1976 he has lent almost $6 billion to 7 million people. One man, one idea.

Bill Gross is the son of a third-generation farmer. He knew that when illness or accident took a farmer away from the fields that a family could lose their entire crop and livelihood. Gross had a history of volunteering for a good cause and eventually decided his calling was to aid farmers in an emergency. With his Farm Rescue non-profit, www.farmrescue.org, Gross, two staff members and over 50 volunteers have assisted over 60 farmers in their time of greatest need. One man, one idea.

In Pakistan, women have traditionally been identified only for their reproductive role in life. Roshaneh Zafar, a Yale-educated Pakistani woman, decided to do something about that belief. With the founding of a group called Kashf, www.grameenfoundation.org, she has been able to lend over $120 million to Pakistani women who use the profits to educate their families. They also enjoy the self esteem of having their own business and being self sufficient. One woman, one idea.

Larry Randall couldn't stand the devastation caused in his Mississippi hometown by Hurricane Katrina, so he and friend Herb Ritchie started the Pearlington Recovery Center, recruited volunteers, tracked down valuable resources and built 400 homes. Bill Drayton, a man with a vision, started Ashoka, www.ashoka.org, a group that assists social entrepreneurs, individuals who seek to create change in their society. Projects are diverse, ring the globe and demonstrate that ideas can be a force for global transformation beginning on the local level.

There are ordinary Americans who have done the extraordinary of giving away half their income every year to help others turn their lives around. Tim and Nancy Nicolai converted four rooms in their Arena Motel in South Dakota for homeless families and have since shared those rooms with over 100 homeless people. Dr. Andrew Moore started Surgery on Sunday, www.surgeryonsunday.org, for people who just couldn't afford necessary surgeries. He has recruited over 300 volunteer health professionals who have performed over 3,000 surgeries free of charge in their home state of Kentucky.

Activist and humanitarian Zainab Salbi founded Women for Women International, www.womenforwomen.org, to give women who survive war the chance to heal and create a new life. Women in eight countries enter a one-year program to learn job skills, business training and to become aware of their rights. Along similar lines, playwright and feminist Eve Ensler started V-Day, www.vday.org, to globally stop violence against women and girls. One of their campaigns is to build a City of Joy in the Congo to assist rape survivors with schooling and trauma therapy.

Nurse Sandra Clarke, spurred by a broken promise to be with a patient when he died, started No One Dies Alone (NODA).

She has organized volunteers and written a manual for the group which operates in 400 hospitals around the world. It is a gift that terminal patients without friends or family can have someone at their bedside when they die. President Bill Clinton wrote Giving and created My Commitment, www.mycommitment.org, to provide opportunities for people to assist change around the world.

Danielle Butin took a vacation to Africa and saw so much need, that when she returned she dedicated herself to gathering surplus medical supplies and getting them to where they were needed most. Outdated equipment like dialysis machines were given a second life in a place with no dialysis machines, instead of ending up in a landfill. Along with scouting out supplies and equipment, she found free transportation to the new facility. She founded Afya, www.afyafoundation.org, and has sent 1,000 tons of equipment and supplies to Africa, Haiti and most recently to earthquake-ravaged Japan. One woman. One idea. Incredible results.

Martha Dudenhoeffer set up a program to help impoverished Peruvian women who ended up in prison because they smuggled cocaine for $35 a kilo to support their families. She encouraged their creativity and skills with handiwork and created Maki (Quechua for hands), www.makiwomen.org, selling the crafts and using the profits for the women's families and for prison upgrades. Rebecca Kousky sells creations of new U.S. designers, www.buildanest.com, and uses the proceeds as microfinance for artisans in Third World countries. Sohini Chakraborty started Kolkata Sanved, an organization dedicated to helping abused women and former child prostitutes in India through dance programs which allow then to release painful memories. So far they have helped over 5,000 women.

Barton Brooks is a guy with a big desire to help. He started Global Colors, www.globalcolors.org , creating grassroots campaigns around the world through donations, volunteers and with local communities and resources. He travels around and tackles projects as he finds them, stocking a small orphanage where the children had been sleeping on the floor, digging a toilet for a Kenyan school or planting saplings in a deforested area in Mozambique.

There are so many opportunities to give. If you can't give of your time, give money. If things are tight, give $5 or give $1. If a million people give $1, the cause will have a million dollars. The Bible says what you give will come back to you tenfold. When I am in a position to donate, I give to many organizations. I am so happy for the people who run refugee camps around the world or ride Zodiac boats to run interference for those trying to kill whales or dolphins. I physically cannot go across the world and climb in a Zodiac and ride rough seas, so I am happy to support those who do. One of my favorite groups is Heifer International, www.heifer.org, which assists people the world over by funding sustainability projects. You choose the project and place to fund, like buying ducks for a village in Thailand. There are projects in Asia, Central and South America, Africa, Eastern Europe and even the United States. You can donate bees, ducks and livestock to stimulate self-sufficiency and you receive updates on the projects and the people involved. When you donate, make sure the organization is reputable and that all donations are used transparently.

I told myself I would not talk about any more African basket charities, but............. I adore baskets. I have always adored baskets. I love their sizes, shapes, patterns, colors and the way they are woven. A psychic once told me that I had been a basket weaver in an ancient past life. I could see that, because I just love them so much. So when I saw the stunning baskets at www.indegoafrica.org, I could not resist. The basketry is created by Rwandan women, striving to provide for their children. The plateau baskets are works of art. I watched a video where the women and children are packing their wares to send to the United States with such pride. They receive computer classes and are taught how to open a bank account. Their humanity shines through, almost as much as their baskets.

Give. Whenever you can and however you can. Flow that energy around the planet and get that serotonin glow.

24

Window to the Soul

The pineal gland is part of our endocrine system. It is a gland the size of a pea, tucked directly in back of our eyes and between the two hemispheres of our brain. You'll find the pineal's pine cone shape depicted in art since ancient times. A huge pine cone sculpture graces a courtyard at the Vatican. Science says it really has no use except to secrete melatonin to assist with sleep and circadian rhythms. Yet it has an extensive vascular system, second only to the vascular system of our kidneys. Our body must think it's important, otherwise it would not have a state of the art vascular system. It is grape size in children, but shrinks with age.

Our pineal gland is our connection to our Higher Self, spiritual realms and other dimensions. It is what is referred to as the third eye. Philosopher Rene Descartes said it is the 'seat of the soul.' It is like a muscle, use it and it will develop. Visualization and meditation stimulate its development. Because of its blood supply, it benefits greatly from deep breathing and the resultant oxygenation. We need to consciously work with it in order to assist our awakening process. Unfortunately, it calcifies with age. In a talk given at the 28th conference of the International Society for Fluoride Research, Dr. Jennifer Luke from the University of Surrey, England, presented her research that the pineal gland is the main point of fluoride accumulation in the body, which is extremely damaging to the pineal. Another presenter, Professor Emeritus Robert Isaacson from New York University at Binghamton, noted that fluoride added to the drinking water of rats created brain changes similar to those found in Alzheimer's disease. Could the fluoride added to city water supplies around the country be the cause of the dramatic increase in Alzheimer's disease throughout our nation? It's also possible that the addition of fluoride to our drinking water supply is a purposeful act to dumb us down and prevent out imminent enlightenment. Protect your pineal gland and possibly worse, avoid fluoride.

Stimulating the regeneration of your pineal gland is possibly the most important thing you can do to assist personal and planetary transformation. It is a locked door to your divinity and power. Your attention is the key that opens the door. Start right now. Sit in a comfortable position and breathe slowly and deeply, until you feel you have shifted into another space. With your eyes closed, imagine your tiny pineal gland straight back from the bridge of your nose into the center of your brain. See that it has a faint glow. Now see the light and love streaming into the planet and imagine that a pure golden, brilliant drop of that light falls onto the pineal gland

and bathes it in luminescence. Feel the warmth of that light inside your head. See that your pineal gland begins to change from a shrunken, calcified state to one of vibrancy and beauty, almost as a lotus unfolding. Sit with that image as long as is comfortable. When you are ready, send love and thanks to your pineal gland and open your eyes. I would suggest you do this meditation at least once a day. As you feel that your pineal gland is changing, you can simply connect with it, flow energy to it and see if you feel anything in return. The veil that separates us from other dimensions is growing thinner, and as we develop our pineal gland, we will perceive much more.

The pineal gland also responds to sound. Sound was an important healing tool in the Egyptian temples of long ago. A study at Taiwan National University showed pineal activity during meditation was more pronounced while the subjects chanted mantras. Musician Tom Kenyon features the Pineal Dimensional Attunement meditation which can be downloaded for personal use, www.tomkenyon.com. Another online meditation appears at www.meditation-techniques.net.

Vibrational remedies are also useful to stimulate the pineal gland. Star Essence, www.staressence.com, offers Pineal Light Infusion flower essence made from the Ellianthus orchid found high in the Peruvian Andes. Its bloom resembles a pine cone and grows in a spiral. The essence cleans and activates the gland, allowing it to expand consciousness.

Work with your sacred pine cone and step into the fullness of who you really are.

25

Matters of the Heart

The heart is more magnificent than given credit for. Most people think of it only as a glorified pump. In reality, it has the largest electromagnetic field of any organ in the body, extending about eight feet from the body. It is very complex with its own nervous system, allowing it to learn and remember. I have read about cases where a transplant patient takes on personality traits and preferences of the heart donor. The heart's nervous system would explain that phenomenon. Its electrical field is 60 times stronger than the brain's and its magnetic field is 5,000 times stronger than the brain's. It forms first in the womb, before the brain.

The HeartMath Institute, www.heartmath.org, is a non-profit organization, dedicated to heart-based living. Their research has shown that love and gratitude create harmony in the heart and between people. They've found that the heart has its own brain, to process intuitive information. It sends signals to the cerebral brain, affecting perception and emotion. Our consciousness not only comes from the brain, but also from the heart. Because of the heart's huge energy field, it establishes a connection and transmits energy between people and their heart fields. You have probably met someone and felt an immediate like or dislike of that person, owing to the connection between your heart fields.

What does this mean to us and evolution of our consciousness? It means we need to be as mindful of our heart as we are of our pineal gland. The two work in tandem, with the heart grounding us in our bodies while the pineal connects us with higher frequencies. When we work with both of them, we will be flowing unconditional love and divinity from our energy field which will affect the planet and those around us.

Take a moment to honor your heart. Close your eyes and put your hand over your heart. Breathe deeply several times until you have shifted into another space. Now imagine the soft pink light of unconditional love, streaming from the heart of the galaxy, entering your body from your crown chakra. It descends around and bathes your heart. Merging with the pink light is gold and white divine light. As you are breathing in the light, send it up and around your pineal gland and back down to your heart in a figure eight, the symbol of infinity. Flow the energy as long as comfortable, bathing both your heart and pineal. Feel the connection between them and the energy spreading throughout your body. When you feel complete, open your eyes. Do this meditation at least once a day to quicken your awakening.

Imagine how powerful it is to have an energy field pulsing with love and divine light as you walk through your world and daily tasks. Work with your energy and flow it out to the rest of the world. The more that you do it and encourage others to do it, the faster we will manifest positive change on the planet.

26

Tap Into It

The Emotional Freedom Technique, EFT, is a clearing tool that activates the meridian system of the body. It is such a simple technique that it is easily dismissed, but I have heard so many people talk about the profound changes in their lives with EFT. Gary Craig, a realtor and a neuro-linguistic programmer, created the technique and now it is used worldwide.

An EFT practitioner will direct a client to make a statement about a negative life situation, such as anger, grief, fear, being overweight or money problems. The possibilities are endless. Then the practitioner teaches a quick and simple tapping technique which allows the energy body to release any blocks associated with that problem. After the negative statement is made, a positive affirmation is said. All the while, the client is tapping the specific acupuncture points. A sample statement would be, 'Even though I have a bad temper and anger easily, I deeply and profoundly accept myself anyway.' One of the most important parts of the therapy is to craft the most precise statement to address the situation or trait which the client wishes to modify. In working with the practitioner and refining the statements, the client might find that the real issue or problem is one that the client never imagined.

For example, I read about a conference attendee that volunteered to work on her weight problem if front of the conference. It started out about her weight issue and her dependence on a certain snack. It ended with her recognition that her mother always offered her that snack when she was too busy to give attention to her daughter. The snack had become the love and attention that her mother failed to give her. With that simple realization, the woman no longer found the need to overeat and lost the weight she struggled with for so long. Remember that our emotions are very powerful and stick in our bodies and chakras until they are released. They need only be acknowledged.

I listened to Carol Look, a clinical social worker who studied with Craig, in a teleseminar. She related how EFT has allowed her clients to progress much faster with life changes than with traditional therapy alone. Research says 60% of people trying EFT for the first time feel a significant change within, while 20% feel better than when they first started. Change happens with a cognitive shift, reframing the problem and looking at it from a new angle. On The View tv show, Whoopi Goldberg recounted that it was tapping therapy that assisted her to overcome a tremendous fear of flying. Whoopi used her tour bus to go everywhere in the United States, and she would take a boat to Europe. After tapping therapy with Dr. Roger Callahan, Whoopi was able to fly to England.

You can experience EFT with a practitioner, through a workshop or with books and dvds. There is a wealth of free information available on the internet, including book downloads and videos to get you started. Craig is now retired but one site in particular, www.EFTuniverse.com, is derived from his work.   I recommend Try It On Everything, a dvd which gives a really clear introduction to the technique.

It is simple and it is free. Tap into it.

27

It's All in the Genes

Our DNA is not only the blueprint for our physical development, but it connects us to who we have been and to who we are becoming. We have all learned in high school biology how DNA works with its chains of nucleic acids and information. It is so much more than that. German researcher Fritz Albert Popp showed that DNA emits light at a very low level, not visible to the naked eye. Slow light waves, soliton waves, constantly circulate in DNA. They allow sending and receiving of information. Russian molecular biologist and physicist Pjotr Garjajev and his colleagues have found that DNA acts like a holographic computer, capable of data storage. Its structure is similar to the structure of the syntax and grammar of human language, suggesting that our language developed in the image of DNA. It has been found to respond to language, explaining why affirmations can be a valuable tool in healing and change. There is a tremendous amount of research available at www.thehealinguniverse.com that is interesting even for a layman about the incredible aspects of DNA.

Of the DNA in our bodies, traditional science says that 90% of that is 'junk' DNA. I find that hard to believe, as evolution ensures that we become an optimum organism. Esoteric tradition says the DNA is our future, now being activated by the photon energy streaming into the planet. It's almost as if the DNA is a 'stargate' between dimensions. There is a double helix nebula almost at the heart of our galaxy, like a mirror – as above, so below – to our evolution in consciousness on earth.

Current spiritual thought says children are being born on the planet with changes in their DNA. They are the Indigo Children, here to assist in the process of our consciousness shift. They are 'wired' differently with a tremendous amount of energy and thus mistakenly thought to have ADHD. Their presence anchors light on the planet and they will begin to remember why they are here. Many are very compassionate and want to help people in any way they can. I have read several stories about children as young as eight years old so desiring to help people, that they have created campaigns that have resulted in large donations for their favorite charity. One young man collected blankets for the homeless in his city.

We are all impacted by the energy flooding into the planet. Higher frequencies can affect strands of DNA which vibrate at a certain speed, bringing them into resonance. We are changing on the cellular level, from carbon-based to crystalline beings. We can work with DNA activation to accelerate our pace of awakening. Activation usually includes a guided meditation or an energy practitioner and then listening to cds with sound created specifically to connect and activate the long dormant DNA. Visionary Music, www.visionarymusic.com offers an information download, a DNA activation meditation and a video at no cost. There are many other sources available on the internet.

When you begin working with your activation, you may feel changes. Your body might go through a detox phase and you may prefer healthier food. You may notice that your intuition is stronger or have a heightened awareness of your surroundings. There is no stopping the energy flow, so the best you can do is to work with the energy and make it yours.

28

Sacred Space

When I was a child, I was very serious and devout. I took to heart everything I learned at Catholic school. I had an altar that I kept on my dresser on a metal tray my mother gave me. It included Jesus, Mary, Joseph and some saints. They sat on a flowered doily and were a reminder of source even at that age.

You might find it helpful to create sacred space at home and work to assist with the changes in your life. Sacred space such as an altar or meditation corner will be a reminder to take time to connect with source. Energy is as important in your surroundings as it is within your body. Everything is one, so if you have stacks of clutter all around, you are blocking your energy the same as having blocked chakras. If you procrastinate reducing your clutter, get someone to help you. Either pay someone or ask an organized friend or family member to start you off. Let go and get the energy moving. Many things probably need to go directly in the trash. Lots can probably be donated to a good cause, sent to resale or sold in a garage sale. Lighten your energy and open the flow for new things to come into your life.

You want to signal the universe that you are ready to change and to clear a space in your consciousness for growth and renewal. Use natural materials, like wood and bamboo. Try to include plants, seashells or quartz crystals which you can program with energy to keep the space energetically pure. If there are religious figures significant to you, include them in the space. It doesn't have to be large and it doesn't have to be expensive. It just has to exist. You can go outside and collect stones and pile them artistically. Include photos, your artwork or any handmade items in the space. It should feel organic, but most important it should feel like you. You can include items you consider special, like antiques or a present from a good friend. Before you start, buy a sage smudge stick to vibrationally cleanse the area. Light it and carefully waft the smoke through the air and into the corners of the room or the area where you have your space. You may want to keep a small glass bowl of water with a fresh white flower for further purification. Bring in a bouquet of flowers or greens from your garden. Include fresh fruit or homemade bread. You can make some changes daily or every few days. Just do what feels right for you.

Make a prayer bundle. Look for an attractive stick or piece of driftwood. Decide on an intention you wish to bring into your life. Write the intention on a piece of paper and roll it or fold it and tie it onto the stick with ribbon, raffia or a leather tie. If you want you can enhance the prayer bundle with beads, shells, paint or whatever else moves your spirit. Place your bundle in the heart of your altar or space and send energy to the intention. Change the intention on a monthly basis if you'd like.

Address the other senses and include sound with music, chimes or a small water fountain. Burn incense or use essential oils to scent the area. Light a candle to bring in the fire element. Spend at least a few minutes each day in your space. Use it for longer meditations if you can. Keep a journal here if you'd like and make it a habit to write for at least ten minutes a day. You can create your own private ritual, an opportunity to connect with your multi-dimensional self.

You can create an area in your garden even if it is only a chair or mat under a tree and some creative landscaping with twigs and stones. At work, honor your space with a reminder of your divinity if it is only a poem, photo or drawing at your desk or taped inside the door of your locker. Bring in something organic, if possible, like a live plant or shells. Honor yourself and your space and you will be honoring all of creation.

29

Music of the Spheres

Sound is vibration and affects our entire being. Throughout the ages, back to Atlantis and tonal healing and as far back as the drumming of prehistoric man, sound has shaped our lives. Today, we can use sound to open an aural highway to our true being. Solfeggio Frequencies are six pure tonal notes from an ancient musical scale which had been long lost until recently. These notes are found in Gregorian chants. The Catholic Church commissioned 150 chants which were used for the faithful to worship in church. These notes have a specific hertz, the number of cycles per second. Research by genetic biochemists shows that note 528hz affects DNA – it can heal and repair the strands. It seems that when the church found that parishioners were experiencing healing and consciousness shifts with the music they were singing in mass, that the chants disappeared about 1050AD. Over the years the musical scale was changed. Today, with the scale we know as concert tuning, the note we know as C is 512hz, while the Solfeggio C is 528hz.

This musical scale was rediscovered by Dr. Joseph Puleo in the 1970s. He was studying the Bible and found a mathematical code which eventually led him to the frequencies. If the Solfeggio tones are played next to metal plates filled with sand, they create symmetrical patterns in the sand. In his book, Healing Codes for the Biological Apocalypse, Leonard Horowitz recounts that Puleo was interviewing a Catholic monsignor who was head of medieval studies at a university in Spokane, Washington. As soon as Puleo asked him the meaning of 'Ut-queant laxis' – the first note of the Solfeggio scale - the cleric ended the interview. Puleo told Horowitz there had been attempts on his life. He said he called a librarian in Spokane who had been helping him with the Solfeggio research, but she said the people she called for information told her to drop her investigation.

Today, many individuals are producing music with the Solfeggio musical scale. Renowned composer Jonathan Goldman has produced several, www.healingsounds.com., with Holy Harmony and The Lost Chord being his most acclaimed. Source Vibrations offer varied selections of Solfeggio music which are directed to specific outcomes such as health, expanding consciousness or creativity, www.sourcevibrations.com.

Solfeggio scale musician Scott Huckabay incorporates the ancient tones into his music. He and researcher Dr. Len Horowitz started Tetrahedron Records, offering Solfeggio music and encouraging musicians to use the Solfeggio scale. Huckabay offers advice to musicians to tune their instruments to the scale. Huckabay and Horowitz believe that by using the Solfeggio tones, humanity can experience harmony amidst a spiritual renaissance.

I downloaded Solfeggio music and played it as I was going to bed. I slept a deep sleep for about seven hours which is very good for me, as I usually sleep only five to six hours. I also listen to the music while I am working on the computer. If you would like to try the tones, you can access free downloads at www.solfeggiotones.com. This ancient scale is another tool to tie in with your DNA and pineal work, and ultimately awakening consciousness.

30

Jo Dunning

Jo Dunning is such a beautiful embodiment of spirit, I needed to dedicate a chapter just to her. I first heard Jo on a teleseminar a few years ago. She is an energy healer with a very interesting story. Many years back, she was yearning to make a strong connection with the divine. She prayed and began saying a silent prayer throughout her day. About two months later, a home intruder shot and killed Jo's roommate and left Jo for dead. But Jo did not die.

After a long recovery, Jo left behind old beliefs and opened to a new way of being. She attended a healing session and found that when she placed her hands on someone, that they were blazing hot and left a red mark on the skin. Then a friend with constant back pain from an accident, asked Jo for help. Jo found she could see into the woman's back like an x-ray and with her eyes energetically adjust the woman's injury so she had no pain. Jo began to work as a healer, and as her practice grew she began to work with groups in order to reach more people. She considers herself a 'modern mystic'. She teaches workshops, does energy healing and carries out speaking engagements.

I knew when I heard her speak for the first time that she is really in tune with the present energetic shift. She has an amazing energy, compassionate and loving. When she did energy healings over the phone or computer, I could sense the energy. I am not one to sense energy. My sister sees and hears things. One day she said that my late uncle Dukey was sitting in the empty chair in my mom's room. I asked how she knew and she said she just knew. I'm not like that. When I have energy work done by a practitioner, though, I do get third eye activation with a lot of movement of shapes and colors. When Jo passes energy during the teleseminars, I can feel it. You might think it's not possible, but remember that there really is no time or space. They are only a construct of our third dimensional beliefs. That is why long distance healing is possible or why a psychic can read you via the phone.

On Jo's website, www.jodunning.com, many opportunities are available. If you can't afford the cds or workshops, she offers a free monthly prayer list where you sign up and she sends you energy daily for a month. She also has a free abundance project with daily energetic support. Twice a month Jo does a free energy session via her webpage. In January she did a DNA activation over the internet, waiving the normal cost of almost $200. I participated in the activation along with almost 30,000 other people. The energy I received in my third eye was very powerful.

Experience Jo's energy as a taste of things to come and align with the new frequencies.

31

There are more things in heaven and earth, Horatio, than are dreamt of in your philosophy.

Hamlet-Shakespeare

When I was a kid, I used to watch the Jetsons cartoons on Saturday mornings with all their space age gizmos. They used to turn on a tv and make a phone call to someone and see them on the tv screen. Now I go into my daughter's bedroom and she is talking by Skype to someone on her computer screen. So I can't really discount anything that seems futuristic, because the future is here.

Incredible things are happening with energy medicine. I read Sanctuary, a novel by Stephen Lewis and Evan Slawson, several years ago. The story centers on a discovery where a computer heals people by sending energy to their photos with hookups from a computer. It sounds far-fetched, but there are computer programs that do it today. Remember that we now live in a quantum world, using the energetic fabric of the universe to create our reality.

Nutri-Energetics System, NES, is a software program for healing. It maps the body-field and indicates any imbalances in the field using a touch pad for the client. The field is made up of magnetic vectors and works with sub-atomic particles. Researcher Peter Fraser, co-author of Decoding the Human Body-Field, spent over 20 years developing the system. After the energy field is evaluated, the practitioner will prescribe infoceuticals. They are bioinformation imprinted on micro-minerals suspended in purified water. They are similar to homeopathic remedies. Both physical and emotional imbalances can be treated. NES also detects early distortions before they manifest. If you visit their website, www.neshealth.com, you can download Quantum Health magazine and a free copy of their new book, Healing Yourself and Others. They also offer music cds which have been imprinted for health. Practitioners in Japan reported that after the earthquake many people had compromised immune systems and the infoceuticals assisted them to regain their health. More energetic healing devices can be found at www.energetic-medicine.net.

I have a friend that uses a SCIO, a similar computer healing program. She did an evaluation on a person and it came up that the bones in the face were broken. It was erroneous, because the client had no broken facial bones. Six months later the client was in a car accident and shattered several facial bones. When we deal with quantum healing, there is no time; past, present and future exist simultaneously.

Yuliya Cohen is an energy healer and creator of the Temporal Quantum Energy Restructuring Technique, TQER. She says when there is a traumatic experience, we can work energetically with the timeline before the incident and then with the future timeline. It creates an energetic bridge and quantum shift to a new reality which bypasses the trauma. She described her group work using the technique with the earthquake in Japan to contain radiation from the damaged nuclear reactors. They focused on seeing the area peaceful and whole before the quake and then seeing the area radiation-free in the future. A new energy potential is created. For more information on the technique, go to www.healingwithouteffort.com.

The future of medicine will be very different, with energy as the primary source for healing. The sooner we become aware of ourselves as energy beings in a sea of energy, the faster we will be able to create our own quantum leap.

32

To forgive is to set a prisoner free
and to discover the prisoner is you.

Lewis B. Smedes

Forgiveness is a simple concept, but it is instrumental to our health and the health of the planet. Blame, judgment, bitterness and resentment are as toxic as any chemical. The energy of those feelings blocks the chakras and makes any true healing impossible. There are places on the planet where whole cultures have created huge energy blocks because of the hatred and resentment they harbor for their neighbors. The list is long down the ages of rivalries between countries, religions, races and even smoldering rancor between North and South in the Civil War. Today hatred continues between rival gangs, political parties and family members.

The first step is to acknowledge the feeling and allow yourself to explore its depth. Many times forgiveness begins with forgiving ourselves. We need to forgive ourselves for not being honest, failing at a relationship, failing at a job, being cruel. As we are all one, when we begin to forgive ourselves, we begin to forgive others. Clearing the energy to allow forgiveness makes space for the new frequencies, like clearing the clutter from your psychic closet.

Whatever you want to clear, whether you want to forgive or you want to be forgiven, remember that you created the situation for a reason. You opened the door and invited it in. Look for the lesson that is there for you. Perhaps it is a mirror. Perhaps you have transformed in some way and become stronger and wiser. Perhaps you should give thanks for the experience. By living in the moment the past will dissolve and the heart will expand into great love.

My sister and I are of Serbian descent. Many years ago we decided to vacation in Turkey. My mother was horrified that we would want to visit a country where 500 years earlier the Turks had ridden into Serbia and cut babies from the bellies of their mothers. That was her ancestral grudge, but it was not ours. And I am sure that same type of grudge exists all around the world. And more are created every day with the horrific gang rapes in the Congo or torture and beatings in repressive regimes.

We must remember that every person carries the God spark within, no matter what. James Redfield, the author of The Celestine Prophecy, says if we look for and focus on the higher self in another's expression, and speak to that part of the person, that the other person can be lifted into a higher awareness. The act of forgiveness can be an act of transformation.

Some of us need to experience things in a tangible way. Write a letter to say you're sorry or write a letter to say you forgive someone. You can send it or you can send it to God and the universe. Burn it over a candle, in the fireplace or a backyard bonfire. But know in that moment that you have transmuted the energy and let go, opening to clarity and lightness.

Taking forgiveness to heart, gospel artist Kevin LeVar started the Forgive and Live Campaign, www.forgiveandlivetoday.org. The goal is to create One Million Acts of Forgiveness. He has received a global response and triggered an outpouring of love around the planet. Decide to forgive and light will flow into all the dark spaces.

33

So Many Resources, So Little Time

There are so many Lightworkers who have enriched my life in many ways. They cover the gamut of topics and offer a wide range of services. I have found them through teleseminars, through my reading or because they just showed up in my inbox. When I first studied spirituality, the only resources available were books, magazines or a workshop here and there. Now I feel blessed that so many people are tuned to the light and so easily accessible.

Marilyn Edwards, www.awakentograce.com is a Holistic health practitioner. She does healing sessions at the equinoxes and solstices and you can register to receive her energy transmission. After her meditation, she sends the very beautiful and perceptive insights she received during the session.

Wynn Free, www.messageaday.net is the author of The Reincarnation of Edgar Cayce. He facilitates several phone calls a week where a person channeling brings in messages from two soul groups of high dimensional beings, the Elohim and the Ra group. It is possible to send in questions about the day's call topic. On Sundays, the call allows participants to put situations such as earthquake victims or wildfires in the light of the circle for healing. You can sign up to his website to receive the daily message.

Sri and Kira, www.SriandKira.com, are favorites of mine. They embody so much light and love that it virtually jumps off the phone line or internet connection. They work tirelessly to offer the latest information about the shift in consciousness and offer free energy attunements over the internet from time to time. I participated in an attunement recently and the energy was strong. They currently live in Guatemala and work closely with the Mayan community.

Another great website is www.greenmaven.com. It's chock full of green news, products and websites from around the planet.

The website, www.lightworks.com, hosts the interesting, informative Monthly Aspectarian Magazine and Astro-Weather, a daily astrological forecast.

Another publication is Awareness Magazine, www.aware-nessmag.com, which offers great articles and interviews.

New Connexion, www.newconnexion.net, is a journal for conscious living.

Michael Mohoric, www.QigongEnergyHealing.com, a really dedicated individual, gifts distance energy healing about once a month. He advises the date and time so you can plan to be in a quiet place to receive the energy he sends. Many people report significant healings after the session.

Beth Budesheim, www.paintedjourneys.com, is an artist who infuses her colorful artwork with energy. She is an intuitive coach, works with energy medicine, and offers transformational courses. She also does personal commissions.

Blue Star, www.bluestarlove.com, is an extremely loving soul dedicated to making beautiful hardwood flutes. He uses red cedar, cherry, mahogany, maple and alder. You don't buy his flutes, you adopt them. They are available in several different keys and he is also working with the 528hz frequency. The flutes are easy to learn to play, and he provides a how-to video. They make a beautiful addition to a sacred space or to use during prayer, healings or drumming circles.

Peggy Black, www.morningmessages.com, channels a soul energy group called The Team which provides enlightened commentary on the vibrational shift and how mankind is progressing. Peggy also does private sessions with the group's assistance.

Steve Rother, www.lightworker.com, channels The Group and publishes Beacons of Light once a month, suggestions on how to navigate the intense energy flooding the planet.

Aluna Joy, www.aluna.joy.com, organizes sacred site pilgrimages specializing in trips to Egypt and Palenque, Mexico. She channels the Star Elders who focus on the transformation that is underway. Aluna had a trip to Egypt already fully booked and paid when the country fell into chaos. As the time grew near, Aluna and the participants decided to take the trip. Aluna's intuition told her they would be safe and it turned out to be a wonderful trip. There were no other tourists, so they had full access to all the archeological sites and the Egyptian people were overjoyed to see anyone visiting their country and showered them with hospitality.

Christine Day, www.christinedayonline.com, author of Pleiadian Initiations of Light, channels Pleiadian energy and offers regular messages, broadcasts sessions and workshops.

World Puja Network, www.worldpuja.org. A great way to stay connected with Lightworkers and the rapid changes occurring in our planetary transformation is to listen to them. They have a fascinating array of interviews each week with high vibrational speakers.

Jim Self, www.masteringalchemy.com, is someone I have recently found who offers a wealth of free resources on his webpage concerning the shift and how to work with the changes and energy.

Mariana Cooper, www.ahamomentsinc.com, is a third generation intuitive and reads the Akashic record, the history of past, present and future. She has an internet radio show, does workshops and coaches entrepreneurs. Mariana is highly tuned to the incoming energy.

Have some fun at www.chicvegan.com, a vibrant site with great resources for raw food, organic textiles and other life-enhancing ideas.

You'll find creative products at www.milkshake.com, where the featured companies offer socially conscious products which benefit charitable causes. Just recently Milkshake provided a petition to sign, initiated by U2's Bono, to bring world leaders' attention to the famine crisis in Somalia.

Ascended Health, www.ascendedhealth.com, offers energetic healing products such as dental care, skin rejuvenation, supplements and probiotics. Two valuable items are the Anti-venom Healing Balm and the Electrical Neopulser. I know a man who had the flesh-eating MRSA bacteria and was told he could lose his arm. He used the Electrical Neopulser and credits it as being instrumental in his recovery. There are photos which chronicle the healing progress of a brown recluse spider bite and a MRSA skin infection.

There is so much out there, all you have to do is open the door.

34

The Mayan Walker

I first learned of Ac Tah, el Caminante Maya – the Mayan Walker – at a lecture almost three years ago. I live in Puerto Vallarta, Mexico and he was lecturing in a small town on the bay. What surprised me was that the information he gave was exactly the type of thing I had been reading in many sources. He said the end of the Mayan calendar signaled a shift in consciousness that would create neural changes in the brain. This information had been passed on to him orally by his grandfather. I was amazed at the timeliness of the message.

About a year later, I heard he was putting together a ceremony to assist Mexico's awakening and to harmonize the energy of the planet. A ceremony was arranged in Vallarta and simultaneously in twelve cities around Mexico. The ceremony takes place on a labyrinth drawn according to sacred Mayan ancestral geometry. It's called El Espejo de Orion – Orion's Mirror. It is drawn in alignment to mathematical points around the planet and the constellation of Orion, with the energy from the drawing extending up to 80 miles, depending on the size of the labyrinth. This alignment creates a high frequency etheric energy field which prepares our electromagnetic field and brain to receive the new energy coming into the planet and raises the planetary vibration. By working with the energy, we can gradually maintain our emotional balance and at the same time expand our consciousness. The Mayans say that participating in the ceremony activates both our DNA and pineal gland.

Within the labyrinth are drawn six circles and a large circle in the center to anchor heart energy. Each circle has a purpose, including meditation, healing, sound, wind, percussion and movement. People volunteer to activate the circles. When I attended, I sat on the ground in the meditation circle to support the energy. Others bring drums for the percussion circle, do yoga and tai chi in the movement circle, play flutes in the wind circle, heal the earth with reiki or another energy method in the healing circle and use crystal bowls and Tibetan bells in the sound circle.

The ceremony begins by everyone creating a circle around the labyrinth and then the passing of a smudge bowl around the circle to cleanse each aura. The indigenous leaders make an offering to the Four Directions from the heart circle and begin the ceremony by blowing a conch shell. Every participant is asked to wear white and to bring a plant and a glass bottle of water. Everyone starts by walking the labyrinth and putting their plant and water into the center heart circle. The people with a task in one of the smaller circles take their places while everyone else continues walking the labyrinth for 40 minutes. At the close of the ceremony, everyone claps for two minutes and then collects their plant and water. The plants are for planting in the garden (if you have one), to anchor the energy of the ceremony into the earth. The water is for drinking to bring the energy into the physical body.

The ceremony creates a very beautiful and intense energy, and it links to the energy created in the other 12 cities. One of the ceremonies that I attended occurred during the rainy season. As more and more people arrived for the ceremony, the sky grew darker and darker. As the ceremony began, it started to rain. It was a huge tropical storm. Lightning split the sky and thunder resonated across the bay. I was sitting on the ground in the large cement plaza and remembering everything I ever heard about staying out of electric storms. The rain was driving and one burst of thunder almost sent me levitating off the ground. I would open my eyes and peek at what was going on, but everyone was participating as usual, although shivering and wet. It was an awesome site to see an elegantly tall man blowing a conch shell to the heavens from the heart of the circle amidst the wind and rain. I put a dome of white light around the ceremony to keep us safe. The ceremony ended and the storm slipped away. We all felt that God, the universe, the Mayan gods and nature had joined the ceremony and intensified the energy and cleansing.

You can create a similar ceremony with family, friends or a group. The labyrinth doesn't have to be mathematically drawn, only to have the intent, as you have learned in other chapters. You can do one in your basement, yard, nearby park or community center. Create the recipe that feels right for your purpose. Add as many elements as you like. Make it fun. The more joy you create in any endeavor, the higher the frequency. Draw the labyrinth in chalk or lay it out with stones or twine. But the most important thing is to just do it. The world is crying out for healing in so many ways, and you can be a part of that. The labyrinth ceremony will focus and harness energy to cleanse and harmonize the planetary vibration. We are part of the whole and can do wondrous things with our minds and intent. We just need to start.

35

Meditate, Meditate, Meditate

When you're buying real estate, location, location, location is the mantra. But when you are co-creating the world, you need to meditate, meditate, meditate. I think my first exposure to meditation was when I was a teenager and the Beatles went to India to study transcendental meditation with the Maharishi Mahesh Yogi. I thought it was weird, but now I know that meditation is one of the most important things that we can do. It connects us with the greater part of ourselves and ultimately to the cosmos. Meditation has been proven to lower stress and adepts have been able to slow their heartbeat and lower their body temperature. It also provides clarity of thought that affects all areas of life.

Studies show that meditation has reduced violence in cities. During the 1990s, quantum physicist John Hagelin asked almost 4,000 Transcendental Meditation practitioners from 81 countries to journey to Washington D.C. He devised an experiment to measure the effects of mass meditation on violence. The participants meditated 20 minutes in the morning and in the evening. During the eight weeks of the experiment, violent crime dropped 24%. Many prisons allow meditation classes, as it lowers violence among the prison population.

During the Lebanese Civil War, Dr. Tony Nader, a physician in a small village in the Chouf mountains began teaching meditation to his patients. They were subjected to constant bombings, as were the surrounding villages. After one percent of the village began meditating, not another bomb fell in the village, while other villages were continuously bombarded. More recently, Sharon Salzberg, a Buddhist Vispassara teacher, led a meditation at the 2008 Democratic National Convention. Meditation is going mainstream.

No matter what meditation method is used, the point is to quiet the mind and create high levels of coherence. Hundreds of companies and organizations offer meditation classes to employees and members, to reduce stress and create health. Hospitals and medical clinics provide mindfulness training to patients for pain control. It is taught to returning veterans to improve their quality of life. Research shows that meditation causes a reduction in migraines, a decline in the stress hormones of adrenaline and cortisol, improved sleep, reduced heart disease, and relaxation, among many other benefits. People who meditate have more DHEA – the youth hormone – than others who don't. So what are you waiting for?

You don't need to take special courses or buy books to get started. All you have to do is sit down twice a day, close your eyes, breathe deeply and empty your mind. Let any thoughts that come in, like what you will have for dinner or what's on tv that night, just come in and then, just as quickly, go out. Keep doing it until you start to energetically feel who you really are. Try it a few minutes twice a day and then go on from there. If you go to www.withinsight.com, they offer 21 meditation exercises to get you started.

Tibetan monks and other long time meditators go into deep delta and theta brain states. Delta brain waves are the slowest and create a dreamless state where cellular healing takes place. Theta waves are slower and allow dreams and creativity. Alpha waves occur during relaxation and visualization. The fastest beta waves signify alertness and concentration. Some meditation cds use binaural beats, a different frequency sound in each ear, to synchronize the brain's hemispheres. Up until now it has taken years of practice to attain that state. In the Monthly Aspectarian, writer Mary Montgomery described a new meditation system which makes it possible to access deep meditative states through brain entrainment. Dr. Jeffrey Thompson of the Center for Neuroacoustic Research, www.neuroacoustic.com, has spent his life developing sound healing for body and mind. His Gamma meditation system allows one to enter a high frequency brainwave state, similar to Tibetan monks who were monitored in clinical studies at the University of

Wisconsin-Madison. The gamma state is associated with shamanic and mystical experiences. His specially mastered cds produce rapid deep meditative states. They are available on his website and you can find more gamma meditations at Sounds True, www.soundstrue.com. Robert Monroe, pioneer in consciousness and out-of-body travel, developed the Hemi-Sync method of meditation. The Monroe Institute offers courses, diverse cds, and even binaural meditations on dvds with visuals of crop circles and sacred geometry, www.monroeinstitute.org.

An erect spine assists meditation with the free flow of energy. Mudras, body positions usually of the fingers, also enhance energy flow. Buddha statues always display a finger mudra. One of the most common mudras is touching the index finger to the thumb. Several mudras are illustrated and explained at www.eclecticenergy.com. If you want to meditate without technology, you may also chant throughout the meditation. An oft used chant is the sacred Sanskrit, 'Om namah shivaya.' One of the many translations is 'I bow to the divine self.' Your meditation will create an energy field with a high vibration and allow you to receive the new energy coming into the planet. It will assist you to gradually maintain emotional balance and to expand your consciousness.

Research indicates that if one percent of the population meditates, it constitutes critical mass and the collective consciousness will respond. Even a group of people can effect change. I remember when I was at a training course in Jamaica and the electricity in half of the hotel had been out for over two days. They were working on it to no avail. Our seminar salon was powered by generator and really hot. I was asked to lead a meditation for the 30 people in the room. We went into meditation and I guided them to see the workers come to the correct solution and connect the power. At the end of several minutes of this focus the lights totally went out and there was an audible gasp. Seconds later, complete power was restored And everyone just sat looking surprised at each other. Coincidence? Maybe.

A few years after that, I was at a training course in Cancun, while category five Hurricane Kenna was bearing down on my hometown of Puerto Vallarta. I asked to lead a meditation for the hurricane. We visualized that the hurricane would lose force and turn away from the coastline into open ocean. By the end of the day we learned that before the hurricane reached Vallarta, it veered away from the coastline. There was not any rain, only high winds and a strong storm surge that did much damage to the downtown malecon, but much devastation had been avoided. Coincidence? Maybe.

We need to learn collectively that what we think in any situation does matter. Whenever I hear of an impending storm somewhere, I visualize that the storm dissipates and moves out to sea. I am sure Lightworkers all over the planet do the same thing. If everyone did that, there is no doubt in my mind that we could control the weather, or at least lessen any damaging forces.

I always had a fantasy that I wanted to lead a meditation on the Larry King Live show on CNN. His show reached millions of viewers around the world. I felt that a meditation involving millions could create change on so many levels. But could you imagine it? What company would want to sponsor a show where the audience had their eyes closed and the screen was silent? Right now it's an insane idea. But we need to change who we are and what we do if we want the world to survive and thrive. We need to have a vision for the future and pursue it with intent, and yes, meditation. Just daydream and imagine the things we could change with worldwide daily meditations. Maybe there is a future where it will be commonplace to do global meditations several times a day, and in doing so to create harmony, light, love and enormous human potential. Now that's meditation!

36

In all things of nature there is
something of the marvelous.

Aristotle

There are times when I smell a fragrance or aroma and I am
transported back to a specific time and place in my life. I
close my eyes and I am there. I used to think of aromatherapy
as just nice smelling oils. I didn't realize that aromatherapy
offers very real healing with science to back up its claims.
Pure essential oils contain phytochemicals such as phenols,
esters, and ketones. When the oils are inhaled, the phyto-
chemical molecules enter our bloodstream carried by the
oxygen and travel throughout the body until they connect
with a receptor. Some oils affect the respiratory system, some
affect the nervous system and some even have the ability to
cross the blood/brain barrier. Once they connect with a
receptor, the molecular structure triggers healing at the
cellular level. It's almost like the CSI television crime show,
where you see a substance rushing through the anatomy of
the body. Because they are concentrated, the oils are 50 to 70
times more potent for healing than the actual plant.

The people in ancient times knew the healing powers of essential oils. They were used in the healing temples of Atlantis and Egypt. There are drawings on the Egyptian temple walls of people smelling lotus blossoms. The oils played an integral part of Egyptian culture, as well as in the embalming process of mummies. The Bible refers to the ritual of anointing over 100 times, and it was described that Jesus was anointed several times with precious oils. The early Christians anointed with oils as a healing method. Royalty has used anointing throughout the ages, especially in coronations.

Today, we can research oils to find a specific remedy for a physical condition like bronchitis or an infection, and we can also find oils which will assist with meditation and higher consciousness. Frankincense was more valued than gold when Christ was born and for that reason was one of the gifts offered by the Wisemen. It is antiseptic and has long been used for cleansing and protection from illness. It assists with grief and depression and aids meditation by inducing slower and deeper breathing.

One of the highest frequency oils is rose oil. It increases energy in the limbic system – the part of the brain associated with memories, emotion, pleasure, fight or flight and motivation. It is a truly spiritual oil and vibrates at 320hz. It resonates with the heart chakra and carries a strong vibration of unconditional love.

Essential oils may be used in electric diffusers, small distillation units or in a ceramic diffuser with water and candle. When my daughter was small and had recurring colds, I would diffuse ravensara at night to combat the virus and open her airways. It was very effective. In the morning when I head down to the ocean, I pick a jasmine blossom and breathe deeply. The fragrance is absolutely intoxicating and really creates a joyful vibration.

You must make sure you are buying pure oils. If they are inexpensive, chances are they have been diluted and will not be effective. They may have been mixed with some cheap harmful additive. Usually the oils are sourced from around the world; Bulgarian rose, ravensara from Madagascar, frankincense from Ethiopia, myrtle from Morocco, neroli from Egypt, cypress from France and eucalyptus from Australia. Wildcrafted oils are available in the United States. They should be used with caution, if at all, with pregnant women and children. Never use an essential oil directly on the skin without a skin test. They are highly volatile and can cause burns. Usually they are mixed with carrier oils like jojoba or sweet almond oil for skin application.

It's fun to sample them in stores or to shop online with the considerable amount of oils and synergistic combinations that are available. Imani, www.imaninatural.com offers great synergies, like Angel – cedar, spruce, orange, tangerine, ylang ylang, juniper, sandalwood, neroli and angelica root! A Chakra Kit with oils and cd is available from www.aureiahproductions.com. One drop of the corresponding oil on a chakra will clear blocked energy. They hand pour all their oils and play high vibrational music while pouring to maintain the frequency of the oils. Yellowstar Essentials, www.yellowstaressentials.com has a beautiful and informative website. They make sure they source their oils from botanical ingredients and their garden. Biblical Essential Oils are available at www.florapathics.com. And www.mountainrose-herbs.com oils are distilled from freshly harvested materials and they offer one of the largest selections of certified organic essential oils in the United States. Aura Cacia produces a complete line of oils and on their website, www.auracacia.com, you can watch a video of the plants being sourced in Sumatra and Madagascar. You feel a connection with the people who are harvesting, and the process which brings the bottle of oil right into your hands. They are also featured at Whole Foods.

Nature has gifted us with such perfection for body, mind, spirit, and all we have to do is to inhale.

37

If you want to find the secrets of the universe, think in terms of energy, frequency and vibration.

Nikola Tesla

Nikola Tesla was a genius before his time. He is an obscure figure now, although in his day he was famous and on the cover of Time magazine. So many things used now, were invented by Tesla. He was born in 1856, the son of a Serbian Orthodox priest, in a region of Croatia. He came to the United States in 1884 after starting his career in Europe as an inventor and electrical engineer. Charles Batchelor wrote an introduction letter for Tesla to Thomas Edison. In it he said, 'I know two great men, one is you and one is this young man.' From that introduction grew a working relationship between the two inventors. Edison worked on the direct current, while Tesla invented the alternating current and tried to encourage Edison to adapt the much more useful current which we use today. They eventually had a falling out and Tesla joined George Westinghouse.

Tesla developed generators, motors and transformers for the alternating current. He held 40 U.S. patents for them which were purchased by Westinghouse. He had over 700 patents around the world. He invented fluorescent lighting, the Tesla coil which is widely used in radios and tvs, remote control, robotics, the laser beam and radio. He had a U.S. patent for the radio and then his patent number was revoked and Marconi was given a patent. Tesla conceived his ideas by visualizing the completed design in all its details. He was bothered by visions which seemed to be ideas of new inventions.

My great grandfather was a friend of Nikola Tesla. They met in New York in the late 1890's, after my great grandfather arrived at Ellis Island with my grandma and her mother. I imagine they met through the Serbian community. My grandmother would recount how the neighbors near Tesla's laboratory would say the ground shook in the neighborhood when Tesla was working on his experiments.

Before his death, Tesla was working on a particle beam weapon, which he tried promoting to the U.S. War Department. He said it would be the weapon to stop all wars. The government was not interested. Tesla invented up until his death. Yet at the end of his life he was considered eccentric due to some of his theories and died alone and without money.

Now you are saying, so what? Why should I care about Nikola Tesla? Because he discovered free energy. In one of Tesla's experiments, he lighted 200 lamps without wires from 25 miles away. He found that the earth could be used as a conductor. By using energy present in the atmosphere, electricity could be produced in unlimited amounts around the globe. Free, no cost. Can you imagine what it would be like to have free energy? Well, corporations of the time did, and they didn't want anything to be free of cost. Mega-financier of the time, J.P. Morgan financed 51% of Tesla's Wardenclyffe Tower facility which was intended to broadcast energy around the world. Morgan asked where they would put the 'meter?' When he found that the energy would be at no cost, he pulled his financing. Later the facility was demolished in 1917 due to alleged World War I security reasons. I believe it was demolished because big business told the government that they didn't want any 'free' energy. Period.

So that's why Tesla is important. There are people working right now to harness energy in the same fashion as Tesla. I am sure the government already knows how to do this. When Tesla died, he left two truckloads and over 150 crates and trunks of his research. The FBI went in and confiscated his research and micro-filmed everything. But, one day the jig will be up and we will have free energy. The truth cannot be hidden forever.

38

A Golden Opportunity

Gold has one of the highest vibrations on the planet. Maybe that's why it has been so highly prized over the millennia. Sleeping Prophet, Edgar Cayce, talked about the vibratory energy of gold in his readings. Monoatomic gold or white powder gold, also known as ormus or ormes, is a high vibrational supplement which has many benefits for the body. Farmer and businessman David Hudson rediscovered ormus, orbitally rearranged monatomic elements, through an alchemical process and holds a patent on the process. Laurence Gardener's book, Lost Secrets of the Sacred Ark, says white gold powder was used by the pharaohs in Egypt and other ancient civilizations where they practiced hyperdimensional physics. He was convinced that the real alchemical secret was not to turn lead into gold, but to turn gold into white powder gold for its amazing properties. Ormus is said to provide mental clarity, improved immune function, expanded consciousness and rapid manifestation.

There are several ways to produce the ormus, including a wet process using seawater and a process using plants. Another process uses the actual metal, although no metallic trace is left in the final product. Ormus has superconductive properties and in a high-spin or high frequency state, is fourth dimensional. It is spiritual biochemistry, affecting energy meridians.

On his webpage, www.subtleenergies.com, leading ormus authority Barry Carter describes the experience of a man taking high-spin ormus over several weeks. The man began to manifest his thoughts, but was concentrating on his fears. If he thought of someone hitting him while driving, a car would come out of nowhere and almost hit him. It became so bad, that he had to sit and do mathematical problems all day so he would not let his mind wander. At night he took sleeping pills. This continued for six months and then began to abate. This was very unusual, as it is very rare to obtain high-spin ormus.

Ascension Alchemy, www.asc-alchemy.com, produces high-spin ormus. It is costly and they are selective as to who they will sell to. They ask potential users to write a letter and explain why they want to take high-spin ormus. They want their ormus to be used for spiritual consciousness. They needed to change the container they were using, as the ormus would ooze through the glass vial it was in and also float within the vial. They use scalar waves to produce the ormus, a technology developed by Nikola Tesla.

I have taken ormus for almost two years and have a great sense of well-being, vitality and coherence. Instructions for making ormus are on the internet and many people produce their own and sell it on Ebay. I have purchased it that way. Although I am a do-it-yourselfer, I draw the line at alchemy. I have used ormus as an emulsion, powder and in capsules. Etherium Gold capsules are available at www.energetic-nutrition.com. Superfood expert David Wolfe has created ormus liquid, www.longevitywarehouse.com.

The most important thing is to research ormus through information and discussion forums available on the internet. Price and potency vary. I have seen ormus priced at more than one hundred dollars and I have bought it for three dollars and it was a good product. Look at several sources before you purchase and read testimonials. Be discerning. The information should resonate with you.

Humanity is experiencing an evolutionary transformation. Many tools are coming to light to assist in this process. Ormus may be one of those tools.

39

Blessings

I've seen a t-shirt that says 'Too blessed to be stressed.' It made me smile and I think it's really true. Unless you're someone living under a bridge in a cardboard box right now, you have blessings to count. If your home is facing foreclosure or you have another hurdle in your life, you may not agree. But you are blessed with every breath you take. You can see, you can hear, taste and smell. Author Sasha Xarrian talked about the considerable hardships and challenges in her life on a teleseminar I listened to. She said, although she didn't understand it at the moment, upon looking back at her challenges she realizes they were all a gift in some way.

She described a very profound, yet simple process that she uses in her life. She puts her hand on her heart and she says, 'I honor myself for...' She fills it in with challenges from her life. Anyone can fill in anything they'd like; I honor myself for surviving breast cancer, I honor myself for surviving sexual abuse, I honor myself for finally seeking divorce. And sit with that some moments until your being absorbs that sentiment.

As you send out blessings to others, blessings will pour into your life. When I see an accident on the street, I immediately send God's white light to surround the scene, to assist the injured and their family, to assist the emergency responders, and in the event of death, to assist that person with the transition and to help the family with their grief. Sometimes I see someone who looks really down and I send them light. It's important to say 'with their permission and for the highest good.' Sometimes things happen for a reason we really can't fathom. I actually was thinking just the other day that I would not be writing this book if I had not been fired from a beloved job that I had given my heart and soul to for 20 years. It has been a long, winding road, but here I am and I'm glad of it. Actually I am thrilled and feel that I am in exactly the right place for me. I never would have imagined it back then.

So bless everyone. Bless those unenlightened drivers that go around like Mad Max, bless hospitals and their patients and health care workers as you drive by, bless schools, prisons and bless everyone on the news. Bless those that have made a violent and unexpected transition, bless the perpetrators and forgive them, bless the people in floods and fires and bless those with opposing political views or those with outright bigotry. You can even infuse your garbage – don't laugh – with light and energy so wherever it ends up, it will in some way, make a difference. When you sit down to eat, bless your food and the farmers and other people who brought it to your table. I am not sure how many people say grace anymore. There is a lovely book, Bless This Food, by Adrian Butash which includes blessings from ancient and modern cultures and religions, like the Buddhists and Native Americans.

Several years ago a group of Tibetan monks was visiting Vallarta. They go from country to country, doing a Tibetan ritual in the place they are visiting, to bring peace and harmony to the planet. Once they were here and did a ceremony in the small sports stadium and another time, they performed their ritual on the Cuale Island. They make their money by doing private ceremonies in local homes. I paid them to come and have a blessing ceremony in my home. They only speak Tibetan, except for one of the monks who speaks a little English. They needed uncooked rice in a bowl, fresh fruit and I put white flowers from the garden in a bowl of water. They conducted a very beautiful blessing ceremony, with chanting and the offerings, and then walked from room to room to bless the house. I was told to put the rice in small bags in every room in the house. The visit was very special and left a sacred energy within the house.

I remember an article I read in a magazine where the author told how one day she was stuck in traffic a long time due to a bad traffic accident. She spent part of the time sending light to the accident site and the victims. Several months later, her doorbell rang and when she answered the door a strange woman was standing there with a bouquet of flowers. She explained that she had been almost killed in a traffic accident months before. After the accident she had left her body and was above the whole accident scene and traffic. She noticed that from one car shone an incredibly beautiful light and that it was directed to her. She noted the license plate number and eventually returned to her body. After several months of recovery, the woman recalled her experience and the license number. At the vehicle department, she tracked down the address that matched the license plate. She wanted to thank the author for her prayers and love. The author was stunned beyond belief.

We are more powerful than we can imagine. Bless everyone. Bless everything.

40

Rock and Roll

My sister recently brought me letters that I had written her over 30 years ago. It was interesting to see where my mind was at the time, and some of the things I don't even remember. In one of the letters, I told her I was reading Jeffrey Goodman's We Are the Earthquake Generation. I hadn't thought about that book in ages, but I do remember that it scared the pants off me. The first earthquake I experienced was a 5.5 quake when I was working in Acapulco in 1981. I was ready to board the next plane home. I know that there are small earthquakes all around the globe every day. Author David Wilcock says earthquake and volcanic activity has increased 300% over the last 30 years. It's the large ones that are worrisome. I feel that the severe earthquakes we have had around the globe are part of the planetary transition we are experiencing. The planet is releasing negativity and seeking balance and renewal.

Dabadi Thaayrohyadi, a spiritual leader of the Otomi Toltec indigenous lineage from Central Mexico, is organizing an 8,000 Sacred Drums ceremony in Toluca, Mexico for the spring equinox in March, 2012, www.8000drums.com. The ceremony is part of a 4,000 year old tradition of his people. The drums represent the beating heart and 8,000 represents infinity. When 8,000 drums beat together, an incredibly powerful healing vibration is created for the earth. Bee colony collapse, drought, mining damage and oil spills cry out for healing. In 2004, Indian nations gathered at the Yellowstone caldera to prevent an eruption. The thousands gathered there prayed, chanted, danced, drummed and created ceremony for four days over an area of 400 miles.

Although cataclysmic earth changes have been predicted, I think we have changed the outcome. Every indication is that enough people have turned to the light to release the need for major disaster. So many people are awakening and dissolving the density around the planet. I am not saying there will not be more earthquakes, but I believe that any movement will be less intense. If you throw a cannonball in water it creates a large displacement of water due to the weight of the metal ball. If you throw one of those sponge balls into the water, it makes a small splash. With less density, vibration is less damaging. And we have a responsibility. Just as the indigenous tribes take responsibility for ceremony around the planet, we need to take responsibility for our thoughts and intention. I do the following meditation every day when I walk down to the ocean. Make it a daily practice and assist the planet with balance.

Center your focus with your breath and visualize the energy streaming to earth from the heart of the galaxy. Visualize it passing through our sun. Open your soul star chakra, about 14 inches above your head and take the energy in through the soul star, filling your body with the energy and then grounding and anchoring the energy. Send it to the molten center of the planet. As the energy connects with the earth's center, see a flash of the sparkling white Godlight permeate the entire interior of the planet. See it pass through the layers of crust, minerals, rivers and caves. Affirm that the light gently loves and heals the planet. Affirm that the brilliant light gently releases pressure and negativity with ease and grace – always with ease and grace. Affirm that the pressure is gently released in the Pacific Ring of Fire, in the New Madrid fault in the center of the United States and all fault lines around the planet. Affirm that pressure is gently released throughout the volcanic system around the planet, with ease and grace. Then take that same light and send it to connect with the light grid around the planet, to send light to every being, human being, place, body of water (see all water pristine), nuclear reactor and radiation around the planet. Then send the love and light out to the universe. I visualize my holographic image above the bay for 24 hours, bringing the light in, sending it into the earth's center, then directing it to the planetary grid and out to the universe. Gently, with ease and grace. So be it and so it is.

41

Vibrational Remedies

Since everything is energy and vibration, some of the most successful remedies are vibrational remedies. They introduce a higher vibration to the body, so the body will entrain or resonate to that vibration. Homeopathy is widely used in Europe and is probably the original vibrational remedy of our time, with 'like cures like.' The cure is found in a substance which causes similar symptoms to the illness. At the prepared dosage, the active ingredient is no longer present in the preparation, although vibrationally, it is there.

Radionics is fascinating. It was developed early in the twentieth century and allowed for long distance healing. Radionics says that every illness has a unique frequency. I have seen it used with my mother. Dr. Martina Goldberg uses radionics at her Holistic Healing Center in Puerto Vallarta. I brought Martina a drop of my mom's blood that I obtained when we did a glucose test. Martina used a pendulum and diagnosed exactly the things that were bothering my mom. I was really amazed at the accuracy of the diagnosis. She prepared solutions similar to homeopathy which greatly assisted my mom's healing. It addressed emotional issues as well as the physical.

One of my favorite vibratory remedies is the flower essence. Flower essences were first used by Dr. Edward Bach in the beginning of the last century. They are made from flowers at the height of their bloom placed in water in the sun to make a mother essence. Later they are combined with spring water and brandy or vinegar to produce a tincture. Drops from the mother essence are then used to prepare dosage bottles. I studied essences with Sabina Pettitt, www.pacificessences.com, in Victoria, British Columbia. Every plant has its signature vibration which creates healing. An essence connects energetically with the patient and can trigger change in body, mind or spirit. It has inherent intelligence and connects precisely where it is needed. Sabina has worked a great deal with Japan, and after the recent earthquake assisted people traumatized by the quake.

In addition to Sabina's essences, I have used essences from www.alaskanessences.com, www.fesflowers.com, www.desert-alchemy.com, www.perelandra-ltd.com, and www.staressence.com in the past. Essences are made around the planet, providing different vibrations depending on their source. I now create my own essences from the many flowering plants in my garden. Rose essence is wonderful for love and the heart chakra and zinnia is one of my favorites, as it brings out the inner child, with a light and playful energy. I often make an essence at an eclipse or solstice to infuse it with an added energy, and under the moon and stars all night. There are people who make them in incredible places, such as under the aurora borealis. Essences can be used by everyone as there are no side effects. A few drops are taken under the tongue or in water several times a day. Many providers also make gem essences from quartz crystal or other stones.

Ann Bliss, totally blind most of her life, formulates essential oils specifically for you, www.youreternalessence.com. She is a healer and channeler who worked with healing energy to regain sight in one of her eyes. She uses her intuition to perfectly calibrate the oils for your highest vibration. You hold the bottle of oil and focus everyday for several minutes. The energy is transmitted through the closed bottle. Healer Bill Dewey says he uses the oils with his clients as they balance energy and speed healing.

Passing energy with the hands or similar means is also very effective. Reiki is a well-known energy technique founded in Japan. Thermal imaging showed the reduction of inflammation during a reiki session. I studied several levels of Universal Energy with Martina, www.universal-energy.net. Universal energy teaches how to access and channel the life force of the universe for personal and planetary healing. Practitioners do not charge for healings, rather it is a service practice. I use it for myself, my family, friends and the planet.

When I see a situation where it would help, I send the energy. Just this week, I used it with Tommy, one of our cats. Tommy came home with his tail terribly injured. I took him to the vet and he gave some medicine for infection and inflammation, but he said the tail was badly damaged and would probably have to be cut off. I gave Tommy his medicine for five days, but I also healed his tail with energy several times a day. At the time I passed the energy, I would visualize that the energy was stimulating the tail cells, reminding them of their purpose, to knit and heal the injury and regain the nerves and movement in the tail. When I took Tommy back to the vet, he was surprised at how much better the tail was. He said I should continue doing whatever it was that I was doing.

Energy can also be accessed through movement, such as with Tai Chi or Qigong. I read that Qigong has cured diabetes and many other serious illnesses. An MRI was done on a Qigong master and it showed that he had energy streaming from his fingers and he could change the flow of energy from one meridian to another. And amazing yoga creates health, vitality and longevity. If you can't afford classes for the disciplines, buy a dvd and make a little time each day for practice.

Chinese medicine is vibrational in the fact that it addresses the five elements – water, earth, air, fire and metal - and how they affect health in the body. Energy and how it flows though the body is an integral part of Chinese medicine, with acupuncture assisting the body with energy flow. Ron Teeguarden, www.dragonherbs.com, offers Chinese herbs and other remedies that are sourced in Bhutan and other hard to reach places in the Himalayas. He is focused on longevity and immune function and has a beautiful, informative website.

Andrew Kemp has created Quantum K healing experience, a 23 minute computer program responsive to healing needs, www.quantumk.co.uk. It features fractal geometry and harmonic sequences with background music. Fibonacci sequences are built in at the subconscious level. The combination stimulates the body to return to its original blueprint. Kemp does not charge for the healing. If someone is grateful for the healing, Kemp asks that a donation be made to his local charity. Testimonials indicate that several people have experienced rapid healing from the program.

One of the most important things we can do right now for ourselves and the planet is to recognize the energetic vibration present in every part of our existence. When we do, we are at the center of creation and transformation.

42

Forget not that the earth delights
to feel your bare feet ...

Kahlil Gibran

Recently I heard Clint Ober, author of Earthing, on a teleseminar. I have discussed the importance of protecting ourselves from EMFs, but his information reveals something as important. Ober was a successful businessman who developed an abscess on his liver which nearly killed him. After surgery and a lengthy recovery, he sold his company and traveled around the United States in an RV for four years. On his sojourn it came to him that electricity is vital to the body. He studied, researched and found that the earth has a negative surface charge and can give or accept electrons. Our bodies, heart and muscles are electrically based and when we connect with the earth, charges are prevented and free radical damage can't happen because the earth donates an electron. The earth is a huge anti-oxidant.

The only problem is that we barely come in contact with the earth anymore, at least not skin to earth. The indigenous people walked barefoot or wore moccasins made of leather. People used to sleep on the ground. At the beginning of the last century, shoes had leather soles. Today 95% of shoes have a plastic bottom. His research shows the correlation between the beginning of the use of artificial soles and the increase of modern-day illnesses like heart disease, diabetes and arthritis. The majority of doctor visits are stress-related, with people being unable to maintain their health due to an over-stimulated nervous system from a lack of grounding. The stress hormone cortisol, also inhibits sleep creating widespread insomnia. The loss of sleep turns the body against itself and can become a major cause of autoimmune diseases like lupus.

Ober devised a system to ground people while they are sleeping through a special sheet and pad which are grounded to the earth through a long cable or plugged into a grounded outlet near the bed. His book and website, www.earthing.com, are full of stories and testimonials from people who experienced rapid recoveries once they began to ground themselves. It's a question of giving the body what it needs and it will heal itself. And if you can't afford the devices to ground you in the home, try to get to a park or someplace you can take off your shoes and make that important connection with the surface charge of the planet.

Another way to connect with the energy of the earth is through dowsing. You may picture someone walking around with a v-shaped tree branch, but dowsing is also done with a pendulum and practiced as a science. I listened to Raymon Grace, www.raymongrace.us, on a teleseminar. He's a mountain man from Virginia who has studied and worked with energy and healing for over 30 years. Grace has studied with Native American medicine men. I read his book, The Future Is Yours-Do Something About It. Grace is practical and down-to-earth. His stories of changes made through his energy work are amazing. He definitely believes that energy follows thought. Grace has created the Energize Your Life dvd that sends focused energy for clearing and healing. One of his clients played the dvd on her tv while she was at work every day for months. In front of her tv, she had a map of her crime-ridden city open on a table. After several months of the map energy work, the local paper headline said crime had fallen to a 30 year low. Some energy problems are created by geopathic stress and that is where the dowsing is especially useful. Grace also works with energy for solving problems throughout the country. On www.raymongraceprojects.com, you can join him if you'd like.

We only have to open to energy and there are so many possibilities for our life and our world.

43

Born Again

Leonard Orr developed the rebirthing breathing technique in 1973. He came upon the method through personal experimentation. He discovered that everyone holds birth trauma within their bodies. During therapy, some people would remember things that happened while they were in the womb, like a fight between their parents. Others would remember trauma from their actual birth. Rebirther Dan Brule, www.breathmastery.com, says we are conditioned from the moment that we are born and those memories are stored within our cells, often causing blockages. Connected breathing moves those blockages.

Our culture is accustomed to shallow breathing. We rarely see our belly rise and fall. Deep breathing is used in many therapies, including meditation. When breathing is connected, it can create an altered state where pain and trauma are breathed out, making space for balance and health. Brule says that 75% of toxins are released through our breath. If we are not breathing properly, we will not be able to release the toxins. Brule stresses that we experience our maximum lung capacity between 20 and 30 years of age. After that it starts to decline. If we don't work to keep our lung capacity up, it seriously affects health and aging.

It is important to have a trained instructor to assist you in the rebirthing process. Many things you can do on your own, but this is not one of them. Because it can cause an altered state, you want to be with someone who has experience facilitating the emotional release. Brule explains that rebirthing can integrate psychological, physical and emotional healing. There can also be profound spiritual experiences. Rebirthing is used in recovery programs and it's also used by athletes and others who want to improve their performance in life. It focuses on the importance of the rhythm, speed and location of our breath. It assists us with our growth and understanding of ourselves.

When I was born, they held my mother's legs together for one hour, so I would not be born without the doctor there. I remember when I was little that I would crawl on top of my dad when he was laying on the living room couch. If I fell and wedged myself between him and the back of the sofa, I would panic. I am super impatient and have always chafed against anything curtailing my freedom. I am sure it stems from the fact that I was ready to be born and had to be in that cramped space for all that time. It makes me shudder to think of it. At some point I will connect with rebirthing.

Brule's passion is spiritual breathing. He says that every breath is a prayer. When we have a beautiful thought or wish, we can attach a breath and send it to the world. Sounds like a plan.

44

Seek Sustainability

I recently heard author/researcher Gregg Braden on a radio show, and one of the most interesting things he said about the shift was that we were never meant to stay at the level of evolution where we are right now. It is only a stepping stone to something sustainable. It really resonated with me. So here are some ideas to create a more sustainable lifestyle for our planet.

Some groups have partnered and are focused on creating sustainability in the desert, www.saharaforestproject.com. They want to optimize food production, use seawater minerals, create green jobs, produce freshwater and have commercial viability. Right now they are working on a demonstration model. If any millionaires/billionaires are reading this, contact them and reclaim the desert.

Part of sustainability is assisting others to survive and be productive. Over one million people are still living in tents in Haiti since the massive earthquake. Artists for Peace and

Justice, www.apjnow.org, is a group of actors and musicians dedicated to building a school for young adults. The first phase is complete and they are seeking funding for the second phase.

You can have naturally clean clothes with Earth's Berries, organic Soap Nuts. They are actually the fruit from the soapberry tree found in India and Nepal. They are known worldwide as a cleaning agent. A $30 two-pound bag of the nuts will replace nine 32oz. bottles of detergent. It will do between 250-350 loads of laundry. The saponins in the nuts do not leave traces on clothes like regular detergent and are gentler so clothes look better longer. They also naturally soften fabric. You put 4-5 of the nuts in a small cotton bag and throw it in with the wash. You can use them several times. There is a way to create a household cleaner or spot remover from the nuts. They are sourced from a small village in India, creating jobs for the village. Buy them at www.ethicalocean.com.

There are so many problems worldwide, but www.globalgiving.com provides a lot of solutions. Since it was founded in 2002, $51,000,000 has been donated to over 4500 projects. They offer 17 categories of projects in five continents around the globe. East African famine is one of their current priorities.

The website, www.theglobalbrillianceproject.com, features social and global innovators who create success and celebration around the world. They encourage people to 'unleash their brilliance' and shine their light through projects and businesses. They have several videos of amazing people and companies around the planet and they offer 'A How to Guide to Visionary Entrepreneurs' on their site.

Sustaining health is also important. I recently found a product that has far reaching health effects. My friend, Sunshine, took MMS, Mineral Miracle Supplement when she went on a group tour to India. She told Dr. Romo before she went that she didn't want to get the anti-malaria vaccination. He suggested she take MMS while on the trip, and she has been taking it ever since. She was the only person on the trip who didn't get sick in some way. She feels it keeps her healthy by taking it on a maintenance basis. I was intrigued because Dr.Romo recommended it, so I have done some research. MMS is the combination of the anti-microbial agent, chlorine dioxide, and citric acid which creates sodium chlorite. Jim Humble discovered its effectiveness, and trials were done in Africa where people were cured of malaria. It also helps with aids, hepatitis, cancer, fungus, bacteria, virus, parasites and heavy metals. On www.healthfreedom.org, you can watch a video with researcher Andreas Kalcker, and there is a free download of information on www.miraclemineral.org.

For people suffering from asthma, bronchitis and lung problems, I have recently learned of Himalayan salt. Himalayan salt is over 200 million years old and contains 85 minerals. It is healthy to use on food, but it is also healthy to inhale. Several companies sell ceramic inhalers with the salt. You breathe in through your mouth and out through your nose. I have read so many testimonials where it significantly reduced COPD. My sister suffers from asthma and allergies, so I encouraged her to buy one. She says it definitely helps. It seems that it cleanses and dries the respiratory system. You can buy them on www.amazon.com, or use a search engine to find alternative health companies.

A sustainable environment also means caring for the animals of the planet. Support groups that protect wild animals and sea life. If at all possible, open your heart and home for a pet or two. It is such a tragedy that so many animals are put to sleep each year, about four million. Can you imagine how many dead animals that is? I have way too many cats and two dogs, but when I find kitties that have been abandoned, I just can't take them to a shelter knowing that the odds are really good that they will be euthanized. I hold the small being in my arms and know that the tiny spirit deserves a life, too. It's not a good idea to buy from pet shops, because they usually come from puppy mills. Adopt shelter animals and give them a chance.

We must also be aware of the assault on the earth's resources. We must control the damage done to the earth through strip mining, fracking, deep sea drilling, pesticides, herbicides, burning the Amazon, industrial farming and on and on. We must make our voice heard through our political leaders and advocacy groups, but more important, we need to hold a vision of the earth healed and pristine.

We can create a beautiful, sustainable planet with a new mind set, love and energy. If not us, then who?

45

John of God

Many years ago I heard about a miracle healer in Brazil. I somehow pictured John of God, in a small hut in the Amazon jungle. I guess that was what my imagination conjured up when I thought of a healer in Brazil. I saw how wrong I was when I actually went to see Joao de Deus – his name in Portuguese – in Brazil. He lives in Abadiania, a small town about two hours from Brazilia. There are 32 entities who heal and work through Joao's body and have been doing so almost his whole life. His center is located on a huge deposit of quartz crystal, which magnifies the already intense spiritual feeling of the place. The town is full of small guesthouses where the faithful stay while they make their pilgrimage to see Joao. His center has a main building with a central meeting room and then two smaller rooms for meditation, or current as it is called. After passing to see Joao, you might be told to sit 'in current' in one of the meditation rooms, to increase the healing power during the meditations. There is a small room where you sit in meditation when Joao says you need psychic surgery.

Joao is available every week from Wednesday to Friday. On Tuesday night, one of the 'casa' guides gives a short briefing to explain the protocol of the center and generally what to expect. On Wednesday morning, the pilgrims line up early in the central hall and prayers are said. When you pass in front of Joao, you are with him only seconds, but the entity present is able to look at you from top to bottom and see exactly what it is that you need. You are told to sit in current or report for psychic surgery. At the end of the day you are offered a delicious vegetable soup prepared by the casa volunteers and blessed by the entities. If you have had surgery, you need to be in your room 24 hours, and you might sleep that entire time, depending on how you feel. If you haven't had surgery, you pass in front of Joao on Thursday or Friday.

My former husband and I were directed to psychic surgery on our first day. I asked to be relieved of knee pain that I had for almost 30 years. Alex asked for help for his battle with alcoholism. They tell you not to be surprised if you start bleeding during the psychic surgery. At the end of the session I started bleeding in my mouth, which really surprised me. Afterward, we were in our room for 24 hours and only left to bring a meal back from the guesthouse kitchen. The reason you need to stay in your room, is that your energy field is wide open and vulnerable after the surgery. When I saw Joao on Friday, I could tell another entity was present in his body as the energy and countenance were totally different.

Crystal baths are available at the casa, where you lie on a massage table with seven quartz crystal points suspended over the chakras with light and color pulsating through the points. The baths help to clear the chakras. Many Brazilians visited the casa when I was there, but there were also people from around the world. There is a room filled with crutches, wheelchairs and eyeglasses that people no longer needed after seeing Joao. People are not only physically healed at the casa, but they are healed of spirit as well. When I stood in line waiting my turn the first day, I heard the two women in front of me saying that a woman with breast cancer had been operated on during the night by the entities. She woke up in the morning with a scar on her breast. The entities can show up at any time and anywhere once you are in Abadiania. The vibration of love is pervasive at the casa, and you are different when you leave than when you arrived.

I never had pain in my knee again after leaving Brazil, and Alex has not had another drink and it has been almost eight years. Energy, love and miracles do exist.

46

Abundance

I would be remiss if I didn't say at least something about abundance. The Secret was about abundance, and there are so many books and workshops on abundance. It has spawned an industry in itself. Now that's abundance! But there must be a missing puzzle piece if so many people still experience lack in their lives.

Back to basics, your thoughts create reality and energy follows thought. So if you are constantly thinking about all your bills and your lack of funds, you are creating more of the same. You are a huge magnet for more bills and more lack. So don't think about them. As soon as you start to go down that road, transmute them into light and start thinking about all the great things you'll do when the faucet opens. When a bit of good luck comes in, look at it as the beginning of the flow and be grateful. Think about a better outcome, see it, feel it, and let your emotions wrap themselves around it. Go into daydream mode and really visualize how the whole thing will be. Taste the lobster dinner you'll have, hear the concert you'll go to and dream the trip you'll take once you switch gears. Be so grateful for the wonderful things that already fill your life. Be enthusiastic and fill your desires with love and energy.

Then follow the Goya Law. I recently listened to abundance expert John Assaraf on a teleseminar. He said you need the Goya Law. I said, well, I don't remember that. I wonder if it has to do with Goya the painter? Then Assaraf said – get off your ass! That's the Goya Law. I bust out laughing at that. He said so many people would email him that they prayed, meditated or visualized all day, but that nothing happened. But you have to have action. You have to do something to get the energy moving. You have to have a plan in addition to the mind work that you do. Assaraf suggests that you create a specific goal, that you plan and have a deadline. Set up a daily ritual. Start with vibration, thinking, planning and finally, doing. Do any little thing to get the energy moving. Look at the want ads, get ideas on the internet, make phone calls, post a note on a supermarket bulletin board or a business card at your local coffee shop.

Keep your expectations and vibration high. That's how you magnetize yourself. With the tremendous amount of energy impacting the planet, we can manifest much faster than ever before. Vallarta is a very difficult town to park a car, but I always find parking. I know I will find a space when I get to where I'm going, and there it is. Remember, you must believe it to see it. And it doesn't hurt to ask your guides for assistance, guideposts and synchronicities. If you're looking for a relationship, you have to get out of the house to find one. You have to go where there are other people. I have a friend that has taught me so much about flow. He is always in the flow and has connected with so many opportunities because he is open to life. It blows my mind. He doesn't immediately throw up roadblocks, instead he entertains the possibility.

That's a good way to end this. Just entertain the possibility. Mull it over and see how it feels. The universe is waiting to give you that and something even better.

47

Crystalline Energy

Quartz crystals are precise energy, used in computers and watches, but they are so much more. They are a form of high frequency consciousness that stores and transmits information and can be used for cleansing, healing, balancing and intensifying energy. They have been branded woo woo in the new age movement, but they are really scientific with their precise energy and piezoelectric properties. The electromagnetic energy inside them is so powerful that when small pieces are run over by vehicles within the mines, flashes of light are released.

I am crazy for crystals and feel that I worked with them in a past life. I am absolutely drawn to them when I see them. I studied crystal healing with author Katrina Raphaell. About 1986 I started to travel to Zacatecas and Guanajuato to visit the mines and buy crystals. I would visit the store at the mine site and also the homes of local miners. I would get the crystals back to Vallarta and then take them to Chicago when I was on vacation and sell them to new age stores. With the money I made, I traveled to Machu Picchu in 1988. When I was in Brazil to see John of God, I almost lost my mind over the incredible crystals that come out of the Brazilian mines.

Crystals are not the only stones that have a certain vibration. All gems vibrate and can be used for so many things in our life. Turquoise is a powerful protector. I remember hearing astrologer Eileen Nauman talk about a friend who had been one of the first people to fly over Chernobyl in a plane. He had a large piece of turquoise in his pocket. The other passenger later became ill and died from the radiation, but Eileen's friend was fine. His turquoise, though, turned black. It had protected him and absorbed the radiation. He returned it to Gaia by burying it in the earth.

Stones are very powerful for chakra balancing. As every chakra has a color, a gem corresponding to the chakra color is placed on the chakra to open, cleanse and revitalize it. Pink stones such as rose quartz or rhodochrosite are used on the heart chakra. Blue stones are used on the throat chakra and so on. Crystal points known as laser wands are used for clearing energy in a room. I have slept with a rutilated quartz in my pillowcase and had amazing dreams. It's helpful to buy a tiny pouch and pick out small stones that influence things you would like to change in your life. Carry the pouch with you, so you bring that vibration into your life. Bring home stones you resonate with and have them in your living space. While writing, I have a fluorite on my desk which assists with thinking, communicating and the assimilation of new information. Cleanse a large crystal point in the sun all day and the moon all night and then program it with your focused intent so it will be directing laser-like energy to the intention. Write your intention on paper and then place the crystal on top of the paper.

The Crystal Bible, a book by Judy Hall, is a great resource for stones. Online there are many sources that sell stones, and explain their use. Steve Rosley, www.crystalmaster.com, travels to Madagascar for many of his stones. He owns a huge crystal skull that he calls Sirius. I have visited his shop in Chicago and sat with my hands on the skull and felt very powerful energy. He travels to different shows around the states throughout the year.

The webpage, www.crystalinks.com, is highly informative with photos and explanations of most stones. Both www.crystal-cure.com and www.healingcrystals.net offer a wide selection of quartz and gemstones. You don't have to spend a lot of money to buy gemstones. If you want a rare specimen, expect to pay a lot, but for small stones prices should be reasonable. Check a few sources before you buy. Many times stores for rock collectors are moderately priced. However you decide to buy, be happy with your stones. Sometimes the stone picks you and you zero in on it and nothing else will do.

Our planet is energetically amazing and just waiting to connect with us.

48

Fear is the path to the Dark Side.

Yoda – Star Wars

It's true. Fear will take you where you don't want to go.
Remember that fear is toxic, shuts down our chakras and
cripples our ability to create the world we want. It's so
important, it deserves a chapter all its own. Fear is
everywhere if we let it be. We're afraid of terrorist attacks,
cancer, financial ruin, criminals, natural disasters and on and
on. It's enough to make you want to pull the covers over your
head and hide. Actually, I did that once many years ago
during a tropical storm. I was living in a hotel and in the
middle of the night I awoke to a storm that had water pouring
into my room from all sides. I looked out the balcony door
and saw the palm trees bent in half and raging rain. I decided
there was nothing to do, so I got in bed and pulled the covers
over my head. Things looked a lot better in the morning.

The funny thing about fear, is that all those things we waste
our time worrying about, just don't happen. I mean, really,
think about it. Think about all the things you have worried

about and how none of them happened. Wasted energy. I feel sad for my mom. So much of her life was spent worrying about everything under the sun. I used to tell her that life is not a tragedy waiting to happen. Yes, tragedies do happen, but rarely. So the best thing to do is to avoid whatever triggers your fear. I'm sure a biggie is watching the news. Very rarely is it good news and lots of times it's fear mongering. And stay away from negative people. The higher you maintain your vibration with love, gratitude and joy, the easier it will be to avoid fear. Now I know that sometimes an idea gets in your head and you just can't shake it no matter what you do. A nagging little worry will just eat away at you and cause a sick feeling in the pit of your stomach. The following meditation is a powerful tool to transmute the fear so you can get on with creating personal and planetary transformation.

St.Germain is an Ascended Master assisting our evolution of consciousness. He gave us the Violet Flame of Transmutation to overcome what we think we just can't handle. It is pure and it is powerful. Different sources say different things, that you have to say certain words or certain prayers, but the only thing that matters is that you work with the flame.

Take a deep breathe and close your eyes. Breathe deeply and rhythmically until you feel you have entered sacred space. Visualize your connection with your third eye pineal gland. As you connect, ask to receive the Violet Flame. See the brilliant violet flame of light descend around you and completely cocoon you in its presence. It is blinding in its intensity, yet you feel safe, protected, soothed. Now release whatever you are holding that does not serve you. If you cannot think of specifics, simply say that you give permission to transmute that which is not for your highest good. Now recognize your fears and put them in front of you in an energetic ball. See their darkness and density. Ask that the violet flame engulf them and transmute them to a higher source. See it happen. Stay in the flame for as long as you like. When you finish, be grateful for the violet flame energy and return it to source. So be it and so it is.

49

Hawaiian Magic

Often in life, the simplest things can be the most profound. That's how it is with ho'oponopono. It's a great way to end this book, because it is so quick and easy. You can make it a part of your life just like that.

About 30 years ago, Dr. Hew Len started as a newly hired clinical psychologist at the Hawaii State Hospital, in a ward for the criminally insane. As a workplace, the staff recounted that it was filled with violence, fear and a threatening atmosphere. Dr. Len did not meet with the patients, rather he was smiling and cheerful as he sat and read their charts. If any staff members were interested, he explained what he was doing. He was practicing a form of an ancient Hawaiian technique. It originally was used to assist on the community level, but Len's teacher, Morrnah Nalamaku Simeona, adapted it for the individual.

Basically, it says that each one of us creates our own reality, thus we are responsible for what exists within that reality, and can change it. For the four years that Len worked at the facility, he silently took responsibility for the murderers and rapists that were his charges. He worked on healing that part of himself that created those patients. As time went on, the threatening atmosphere dissolved and patients no longer were shackled or needed so many drugs. The staff stopped calling in sick and changes were made around the facility, including painting and gardening. Little by little the prisoners were healed and released, until only two patients remained. They were transferred and the facility was closed.

Len says that he healed the part of himself that had created the criminally insane. So the process goes that you need to acknowledge that everything is your creation, ask source to heal it and then thank the process. Mabel Katz, a student of Len's, offers a lot of information and radio interviews at www.mabelkatz.com.

The most important thing is that you do it, starting today and make it a part of your life. I have read so many testimonials about this simple technique, and how it has brought amazing change into people's lives. Say it to yourself, say it silently to someone else, say it to the world. I have seen the words in different orders, but the way I learned is to say, 'I'm sorry, please forgive me, I love you, thank you.' Simple, yet profound. Let's step into the light and change the world.

I'm sorry.
Please forgive me.
I love you.
Thank you.

Not the End, Just the Beginning

I hope I have passed on something of value, something to make the way a bit easier. Avoid fear at all costs. It is a normal reaction, but limiting and destructive. As soon as you feel fear, send it to the light and transmute it. Recognize the value in every moment to create the world and future you want. Your thoughts, feelings and emotions create reality and you have chosen to be here to do just that, to create a reality that is beyond anything that you have imagined. Be present in your heart and feel the connection between you and the rest of the world. The universe is complex and infinitely beautiful. You carry a universe within you. Love it. Be it. Shine it. I can say no more. Much love to you.

Nothing
else in the
world, not
all the
armies,
is so
powerful
as an idea
whose
time has
come.

Victor Hugo

ABOUT THE AUTHOR

Chris Sausser lives in Puerto Vallarta, Mexico with a deep and abiding love for the planet and all her inhabitants. Her greatest desire is to assist the transformation to the light. You can contact her at:

planetarytransformation@gmail.com.

www.chrissausser.com

NOTE

Chris did not receive anything from anyone to mention them in the book. All recommendations came from the heart, with the intent for the highest good. Besides, as her dad used to say, they don't know her from a load of hay!